When the ADHD Diagnosis Is Wrong

D0076883

When the ADHD Diagnosis Is Wrong

Understanding Other Factors That Affect Attention in Children

Paul G. Swingle, PhD

 PRAEGER™

An Imprint of ABC-CLIO, LLC
Santa Barbara, California • Denver, Colorado

DiPietro Library
Franklin Pierce University
Rindge, NH 03461

Copyright © 2015 by Paul G. Swingle

All rights reserved. No part of this publication may be reproduced, stored in a retrieval system, or transmitted, in any form or by any means, electronic, mechanical, photocopying, recording, or otherwise, except for the inclusion of brief quotations in a review, without prior permission in writing from the publisher.

Library of Congress Cataloging-in-Publication Data

Swingle, Paul G.
    When the ADHD diagnosis is wrong : understanding other factors that affect attention in children / Paul G. Swingle, PhD.
        pages cm
    Includes index.
    ISBN 978-1-4408-4066-1 (hardback) — ISBN 978-1-4408-4067-8 (ebook)
    1. Attention-deficit hyperactivity disorder—Diagnosis.   2. Attention-deficit hyperactivity disorder—Treatment.   I. Title.
    RJ506.H9S95 2015
    618.92'8589—dc23   2015015197

ISBN: 978-1-4408-4066-1
EISBN: 978-1-4408-4067-8

19 18 17 16 15   1 2 3 4 5

This book is also available on the World Wide Web as an eBook.
Visit www.abc-clio.com for details.

Praeger
An Imprint of ABC-CLIO, LLC

ABC-CLIO, LLC
130 Cremona Drive, P.O. Box 1911
Santa Barbara, California 93116-1911

This book is printed on acid-free paper ∞

Manufactured in the United States of America

This book discusses treatments (including types of medication and mental health therapies), diagnostic tests for various symptoms and mental health disorders, and organizations. The authors have made every effort to present accurate and up-to-date information. However, the information in this book is not intended to recommend or endorse particular treatments or organizations, or substitute for the care or medical advice of a qualified health professional, or used to alter any medical therapy without a medical doctor's advice. Specific situations may require specific therapeutic approaches not included in this book. For those reasons, we recommend that readers follow the advice of qualified health care professionals directly involved in their care. Readers who suspect they may have specific medical problems should consult a physician about any suggestions made in this book.

Contents

INTRODUCTION

Treat the Condition Not the Label

The main reason for writing this book is not because we need yet another book on Attention Deficit Hyperactivity Disorder. I wrote this book because I am alarmed. It has become apparent that we are becoming intolerant of normal children's behavior. We do not recognize the emotional challenges that many children have in our culture and we, as parents, often do not take responsibility for the tensions we create that our children must endure.

A study published in the *Journal of the American Academy of Child & Adolescent Psychiatry* by Dr. Susanna Visser and her colleagues (November 2013) reported that a total of 11 percent of 4- through 17-year-olds had received a diagnosis of ADHD by a health care provider. This represents a 42 percent increase in the diagnosis of ADHD from 2003/2004 to 2011/2012! Six percent of these children were reported by their parents to be taking medication for ADHD, a 28 percent increase from 2007/2008 to 2011/2012.

Attention Deficit Disorder and Attention Deficit Hyperactivity Disorder—technically, ADHD (Inattentive, or ADD) and ADHD (Hyperactive, or ADHD)—are real disorders. They cause considerable difficulty for children (and their families), and the sooner in life the conditions are treated, the better. So, although I will be reviewing all the various forms of AD(H)D, much of this book will be addressing the other reasons for children's inattentiveness and other emotional/behavioral problems. AD(H)D has become a wastebasket diagnosis in which any child with a focusing problem is thrown into this diagnostic catchall and then medicated. The number of children being medicated for school-related problems in some locales is staggering (but not surprising given that in the United States, one out of every five individuals is taking a psychotropic medication! It is no small wonder then that we are becoming intolerant of normal children's behavior and medicating them because we prefer not to deal with normal children.

The second reason for writing this book is that in the Swingle Clinic we are seeing many children who are diagnosed with ADHD but have other reasons for their inattentiveness and/or hyperactivity. These children often have stressful situations such as bullying or family strife that interfere with their ability to be attentive. They are often hyperactive because they are anxious or frightened. Medicating these children with attention-enhancing medications usually exacerbates their condition, so by process of trial and error, the medications evolve into antidepressants, anxiolytics, or antipsychotics. This is a tragedy, simply stated.

There are compelling reasons to encourage proper assessment of the conditions associated with the attention/hyperactivity problem rather than simply look at the symptoms. The symptoms of fear may mimic ADHD, leading to a misdiagnosis of ADHD and totally inappropriate treatments. The inappropriate treatments may be pharmaceutical or psychological, but they are ineffective because they are determined by symptoms, not causes. The irrationality of this approach is nicely captured by the diagnostic criteria used for applying the labels of ADHD (Inattentive Type, see Table I.1), ADHD (Hyperactive Type, see Table I.2) advocated in one of the diagnostic manuals (*Diagnostic and Statistical Manual of Mental Disorders— DSM-IV*). There are other such nosologies that are equally illogical.

Table I.1   Diagnostic Criteria for Attention Deficit Hyperactivity Disorder, Inattentive Type

Six or more of following for at least six months

1. Fails to give close attention to details or makes careless mistakes
2. Difficulty sustaining attention in tasks or play
3. Does not seem to listen when spoken to directly
4. Does not follow through on instructions and fails to finish tasks
5. Difficulty organizing tasks and activities
6. Dislikes or avoids tasks that require sustained mental effort
7. Loses things necessary for tasks or activities
8. Easily distracted by extraneous stimuli
9. Forgetful in daily activities

So, here are a few questions about these criteria. First: What if you only have five of the criteria? Or three? What if the parent notices these behaviors

Table I.2   Diagnostic Criteria for Attention Deficit Disorder, Hyperactive Type

Six or more of following for at least six months

1. Fidgets and/or squirms
2. Leaves seat when remaining in seat is expected
3. Runs /climbs excessively: with adults, reports subjective feelings of restlessness
4. Difficulty playing or engaging in leisure activities quietly
5. "On the go" or acts "driven"
6. Talks excessively

Impulsivity

1. Blurts out answers before questions completed
2. Has difficulty waiting turn
3. Interrupts or intrudes on others

and has observed them for three months—not yet ADHD? Let Johnny fail his semester since we have to wait six months for it to be REAL ADHD? What if you only observe these behaviors in church? And will someone please let me know what is meant by a child "running or climbing EXCESSIVELY!" I should note that in a more recent version of the diagnostic manual (DSM-5), this has been changed to "inappropriately."

It is clear that this system is not very helpful. The system provides a name for a presumed disorder. The name does not provide any information. It does not give guidance for what to do to fix the problem. A major problem with our health care system is that we have a huge industry devoted to naming disorders. This is true in all areas of the health care industry.

It is interesting to note a recent study by Dr. Daniel Safer and colleagues published in the *Journal of the American Medical Association: Psychiatry* (2015) found that there has been a marked increase in the NOS (not otherwise specified) diagnoses with children for exactly the reasons just stated. That is, children who do not meet all the criteria for the label are given the subthreshold (shadow) designations. This can be a problem because of inappropriate off-label prescribing and the creation of a "vast heterogeneity" of disorders that confounds research into effective treatment methods.

Parents arrive in my office with huge files containing the results of days of testing that provide little useful information about how to deal with their child's problem(s). So, with ADHD we have many books and treatment programs designed to help the child cope with his/her problem and to help parents cope with their child's problem. The danger of these approaches is that it distracts from the main issue of treating the cause of the problems. If it is ADHD then there are neurological conditions associated with those problems that can be treated. If the problems stem from other circumstances such as bullying or family conflict then neurological assessment can identify this possibility and therefore focus therapy in a relevant direction.

There are therapists who are quite talented in uncovering conditions such as family strife that may be at the root of the child's academic problems. However, rather than waste time and money searching out these possibilities in the context of presumed ADHD, it is far more efficient to determine the neurological conditions that identify the various forms of ADHD and also discriminate between conditions of ADHD and many other conditions that can affect children's behavior.

In this book I will address the neurological basis for the reasons that a child cannot pay attention in school. Some of these are, in fact, what one might legitimately call ADD or ADHD. I will also review a number of conditions in brain functioning that, although they interfere with a child's ability to sustain attention and focus, are not ADD. These conditions are often associated with severe stress, such as in some forms of bullying, family strife, emotional disturbances, sleep problems, and conditions that are associated with poor stress tolerance.

We have known for some time that many children of alcoholics show a deficiency in the ratio of slow frequency amplitude to fast frequency amplitude of brainwave activity in certain regions of the brain. With adults, this condition (low Theta/Beta ratio—much more detail about this later) gives rise to poor stress tolerance, predisposition to anxiety, sleep quality problems, self-medicating behavior, and often feelings of fatigue and depression. The person cannot find a switch to turn the brain off and alcohol helps the individual quiet the hyperactive brain.

In the young child, this deficiency in the Theta/Beta ratio gives rise to a lot of chatter in the brain and the chatter is interfering with the child's ability to focus. There is just too much going on in the head so the child can neither focus nor stay put. This is one of the conditions that if defined as ADHD is often medicated with a stimulant. This method of treating this condition exacerbates the condition, as one might expect. The problem is that the brain is overly active. There is too much chatter, thus a central nervous system stimulant may increase that chatter and hence exacerbate the problem.

Another example is children of depressed parents, particularly the mother. A number of researchers have found that children of depressed mothers are more likely to have an imbalance in the frontal regions of the brain that is associated with predisposition to depression. Children with this predisposition would be expected to be vulnerable to depression and more likely to respond to environmental triggers by manifesting disturbances in mood. Depression can have effects other than frank sadness and, in the case of a child, this may include lack of interest and motivation, behaviors that are associated with attention deficiencies.

Although we may expect a genetic link between the mother and child, there are other factors associated with a child's exposure to depressed parents. The first issue is that depressed parents are often not available emotionally to the child. So the child feels isolated, lonely, and not emotionally secure. There is also a dual risk factor in the sense that a child of a depressed parent may have a genetic predisposition to depressed mood states, and being exposed to a depressed parent who is not available to the child emotionally may activate or manifest the genetic predisposition to depression. This is the dual risk model in which children of depressed parents have not only a genetic predisposition but also a high probability of being exposed to a depressed parent, which may in turn activate their own predisposition to depression.

It has also been reported that the effect of maternal depression can also occur prenatally. A study by Dr. Anne Rifkin-Graboi and colleagues reported in *Biological Psychiatry* (December 2013) found that the interconnectivity of the right amygdala (roughly behind the right eye in the frontal part of the brain) was found to be abnormal in newborns of mothers with high levels of depression symptoms. This abnormality in "wiring" was determined by magnetic resonance imaging (MRI) scans within two weeks of birth! Abnormal amygdala functioning is found with mood and anxiety disorders.

When a child is brought to the clinic for treatment of any condition, we start with the intake neurological assessment that measures brainwave activity. The instrument used to determine brain functioning is the electroencephalogram (EEG). The brainwave activity, measured with the EEG, looks at brain functioning as opposed to other brain scanning devices that look at brain structure. The brain activity measured with the EEG is then digitized so that the various measures are presented numerically and referred to as a Quantitative EEG (QEEG).

The intake ClinicalQ, as it is called, is a QEEG based on clinical norms (that is, the comparison profiles are those of actual patients with self-reported conditions). So we have norms for people (adults and children) with depression, sleep disturbance, attention problems, autism, and the like. As you will see, the ClinicalQ tells us everything we need to know about the condition of the client and, more importantly, where to go in the brain to fix the problem.

Before concluding this introduction, I should point out that although the focus of this book is on children, similar and often more serious problems that compromise efficient functioning, including ADHD, confront adults. With adults, it is particularly important to ask: Are you sure it's not ADHD? As we will see, there are many conditions that are badly misdiagnosed and treated inappropriately that are actually ADHD conditions. Depression is a common misdiagnosis for a form of ADHD that affects a person's ability to maintain cognitive and emotional regulation. The person becomes distraught and disheartened because of the inability to function effectively at school or work and develops a reactive depression. Reactive depression is not a condition that one should treat with antidepressant medications or the insane pharmacological cocktails that we see in practice. We will have more to say about this later in the book but for now a good example or reactive depression is the depressed state one SHOULD be in when a loved one dies. Medicating this form of depression is completely inappropriate. You are supposed to feel sad and go through the grieving process. Numbing it away pharmaceutically often means you will have a very long, even lifetime, problem with angst and depression that does not respond well to treatment.

ONE

The Brain Tells Us Everything!

The silliness of going from symptoms to diagnosis to treatments based on trial and error is completely avoided if we follow the dictum *primum non nocere* (first do no harm) by going from bottom-up rather than from top-down.

Top-down leads to trial-and-error treatment strategies with, of course, the potential for harm. Like the checklists shown in the introductory chapter, selecting behaviors from the menu does not help to identify the potential causes for those behaviors. Further, we aggrandize the process by equating behaviors with symptoms. This, in turn, justifies the practice of medicating behavior because one has called the behavior a "symptom." The ultimate obscenity in this process is that we start to define normal, but perhaps strident, behavior as symptomatic and evidence for a disease (recall, six behaviors from the list and you have ADHD "DISORDER") that legitimatizes medicating. We medicate the rambunctious child because WE cannot tolerate their behavior. This situation is nicely captured by a father's Twitter response to an *Esquire* (April 2014) article ("The Drugging of the American Boy") by Ryan D'Agostino. This man, drugged as a young child and "hated being medicated," twitted "will never put my kids on anything for *being a kid*" (italics added).

So top-down is when the therapist/physician/psychologist finds reasons to define the condition (e.g., depression, ADHD) based on self-reports, observations, and expert opinion and then applies canned treatments on a trial-and-error basis until the patient/client reports benefit (or gives up), or the teacher feels better, or the parent can get some sleep.

Bottom-up is when we look at the neurological conditions. Based on anomalies in brain functioning, we ask the client if he/she experiences any of the symptoms associated with the observed inefficiencies in brain functioning. This process is nicely described by Susan Olding in her book entitled "Pathologies" in which she describes a mother's trials and tribulations associated with trying to get adequate care for her child. The following is an excerpt from the chapter in which she describes the process for recording the ClinicalQ and the immediate feedback this assessment provides about her daughter's condition.

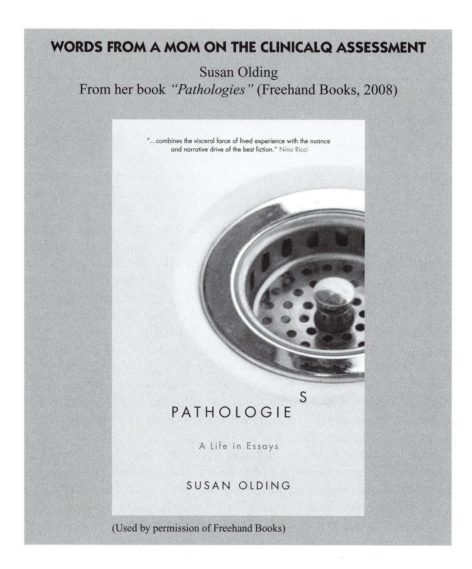

WORDS FROM A MOM ON THE CLINICALQ ASSESSMENT

Susan Olding

From her book *"Pathologies"* (Freehand Books, 2008)

"...combines the visceral force of lived experience with the nuance and narrative drive of the best fiction." Nino Ricci

PATHOLOGIE S

A Life in Essays

SUSAN OLDING

(Used by permission of Freehand Books)

Desperate, determined, undeterred by cost or lack of insurance coverage, undismayed by the doubts of conventional physicians, undaunted by the practitioner's Dickensian-sounding name, I switched off my cell phone at the threshold of Dr. Swingle's office and carried my daughter across. . . .

I had brought a medical and developmental history—the long litany of concerns that had brought us to his door—but Dr. Swingle waved the papers aside without even looking at them. Instead, he ushered Maia toward a computer screen on the other side of the room and told her to put her feet on the stool below. Then he fixed a couple of delicate wires to her ears. . . .

Then Dr. Swingle sent Maia to the "treasure chest" in the waiting room. He stared at the printout in his hand. "Here," he said, and he pointed to an outline of the brain, "these numbers imply trauma." He shrugged, palms up, waiting for my response. I nodded. "And here," he continued, "too much Theta. This is the hyperactivity people associate with ADHD. But it's minor. In the ballpark I play in, she barely makes the field." There was more: extreme stubbornness, a tendency to perseverate, lapses of short-term memory, attachment disorder, inability to read social cues, emotional reactivity, tantrums, explosions. One by one he read the ratios, divining[1] my daughter's character—more quickly, more accurately than any professional I'd yet encountered.

---

[1] Although I am flattered by the divine reference, I believe that Susan meant the more secular meaning: *Divination* can be seen as a systematic method with which to organize what appear to be disjointed, random facets of existence such that they provide insight into a problem at hand.

THE BRAIN MAP

I like to call the intake QEEG a "brain map." Not only does this brain wave assessment tell me what problems are likely the reasons that the person is sitting in my office, but it tells me where to go to correct the problems. Hence the term "map."

As most readers know, the EEG measures the electrical activity of the brain. This activity is measured as a wave form, hence the term *brain wave*. Brain waves reflect the activity of the brain cells and the generators of the brain wave activity at specific scalp locations reflect the activity of cortical (surface) and subcortical (interior) regions of the brain. The level of sophistication and accuracy of this procedure has advanced explosively during my professional lifetime and the precision of this technology is truly astounding. In later chapters we will look at a few examples of highly sophisticated brain assessments that we use for brain trauma, psychoses, seizure disorders, and the like.

For most situations, less complicated and involved neurological assessments are used and this is certainly the case with ADHD and all of the conditions that mimic these behaviors that so befuddle many practitioners. We start with the brain wave. Measured with simple electrodes attached to the scalp, the observed "raw" signal is actually composed of many different brain waves. The basic brain waves are shown in Figures 1.1–1.4. Figure 1.1 shows the spectral display of the amplitude of brain waves from 1 to 40 Hz.

Figure 1.1   The spectral display of the amplitude (electrical strength) of brain waves that are 1 Hertz (Hz) wide. At the extreme left the display starts with 0.5 Hz (1 cycle every two seconds) and then continues at 1 Hz intervals 2, 3, 4, ... up to 40 Hz (40 Hz is 40 cycles per second). Brain waves are grouped based on similarity of function so brain waves from 3 to 7 Hz are called "Theta," 8 to 12 Hz are "Alpha," and 16 to 25 Hz are "Beta."

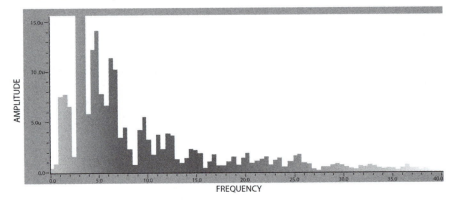

As demonstrated in Figures 1.2–1.4 the extracted brain wave bands Theta, Alpha, and Beta differ in appearance. Theta brain waves, shown in Figure 1.2, are slow, between 3–7 cycles per second (Hz). Theta brain waves generally reflect slowing of activity of an area in the brain, but it depends where in the brain you are taking the measurements. As will become obvious when we examine the brain maps of children with various conditions, the implication of elevated Theta amplitude can differ substantially from brain site to brain site. However, in general, we can say that increasing the strength (amplitude) of Theta can have a relaxing effect.

Figure 1.2   Theta waves are between 3 and 7 Hz as shown here as the slow undulations under the higher frequency surface brain waves

Alpha brain waves are a bit faster, from 8–12 Hz, and have rhythmic patterns such as those shown in Figure 1.3. Alpha is a hugely important brain wave. It tells us a very great deal about the person. Alpha "up" training, which means increasing the amplitude of Alpha, is used as relaxation training. However, as we shall see, Alpha is far more important than just helping a person to relax. Alpha waves are associated with creativity and relaxation but when excessive or deficient in certain brain regions can result in conditions such as AD(H)D, depression, and in some cases, severe emotional and cognitive dysregulation.

Figure 1.3   Wave patterns for Alpha (8–12 Hz)

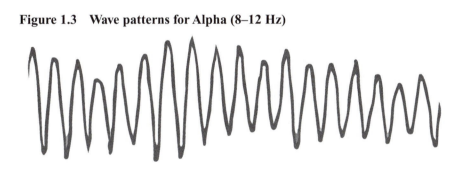

Figure 1.4   Wave patterns for Beta (16–25 Hz)

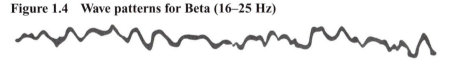

Beta waves, as shown in Figure 1.4, are between 16–25 Hz and have a more ragged look than Alpha waves. Beta brain waves are very fast waves in the brain; Beta activity becomes strong when the area of the brain is activated. In certain areas it will increase in amplitude when one is attentive and concentration is focused. In other areas of the brain, elevated Beta amplitude is associated with anxiety or excitement.

Figure 1.5   10–20 international EEG site location system. The five-point ClinicalQ locations are circled

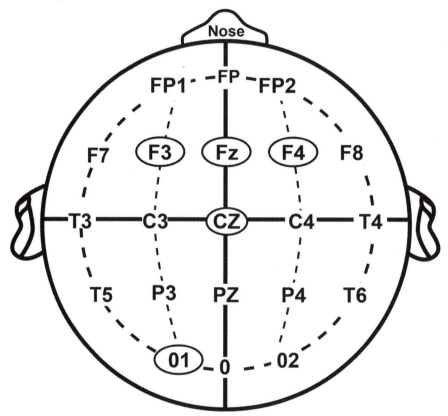

As shown in Figure 1.5, the electrode (measurement) sites are standardized. The assessment used for clinical assessment of children brought in for treatment of learning, attention, and emotional/behavioral problems are indicated by the circled sites.

To illustrate the bottom up assessment procedure, as described by Susan Olding in the excerpt from her book cited earlier, consider the following data from an actual client. As emphasized by Olding when I assessed her child, I knew nothing about this child other than he was 14 years old and not at all happy about having been dragged into my office by his mother. Let's call him Mitch, not his actual name, of course. As noted in the schematic shown in Figure 1.5, the numbers are from five brain locations: the top of the head (Cz); the back of the head (O1); and the left (F3), right (F4), and middle (Fz) of the front of the head. The measurement requires just over six minutes of recording time and the tasks are simple (open and close the eyes and read something out loud).

In our workshops teaching other clinicians to use the clinical QEEG procedure, we always emphasize that neurotherapy is not a standalone procedure. In short, I tell clinicians "Don't leave your clinical hat at the door when you do neurotherapy." During the first session with this child, for example, all I had to do was look at him to know that he was experiencing difficulties. He was sullen and would not make eye contact with me. He slouched in the chair, looking as disinterested as he could, looking out the window and yawning. His mother was anxious to tell me all about his difficulties.

It is very important in these circumstances not to validate the child's expectations. What this child was expecting was for his mother to go through her tale of woe telling me all of the difficulties that the child has had and all of the difficulty she and/or the family has had with regard to the behavior of this child. As described in Olding's account of her experience with the ClinicalQ, I did not permit the mother to proceed with her description of the child's behavior; rather, I addressed the child directly.

Often with young children, if you address the issue of sports, you can start to develop some sort of relationship. In this case, I asked the child what sports he played and I was very fortunate that he mentioned soccer. This provided me with my first possible inroad to being able to get this child to acknowledge his difficulties and address the problems. I pointed out that many members on the team that had won the World Cup in soccer in the year 2006 (players from the Milan team) had done neurotherapy—the same therapy with which he was likely to be involved. I went on to describe some of the other uses of neurofeedback, including its use with a local hockey team and the Olympic athletes who were going to participate in the 2010 Winter Olympics in Vancouver, Canada. At this point the child was attentive to me but still rather solemn and not responding with anything but grunts and head nods.

After this brief introduction, I brought the child over to the area where we do the brain assessment and simply told him that he would feel nothing, that this was measurement only, and that it would not take much time. I also pointed out that I would be asking him to open and close his eyes at various times, and to read something out loud. I explained that the measurement is movement-sensitive and to try to be as still as possible during the measurement procedure. The raw data shown in Figure 1.6 is the result of that assessment. The raw data consists of 99 numbers and these 99 numbers are reduced to 21 summary markers that are shown in Figure 1.7.

Figure 1.6   Raw data from ClinicalQ recording of a 14-year-old male

MALE - 14 YEARS OLD

TRIAL #	THETA	ALPHA	BETA	
1	21.1	12.8	8.0	
2	19.4	15.0	6.3	
3	29.0	19.5	8.6	
4	22.1	14.8	7.4	
5	18.3	13.0	8.5	CZ
6	23.5	12.1	7.6	
7	20.4	12.5	8.0	
8	19.1	12.1	8.9	
9	20.4	13.2	8.2	
10	19.9	15.8	7.2	
SESSION AVG.	21.3	14.1	7.9	

TRIAL #	THETA	ALPHA	BETA	
1	17.8	16.2	7.5	
2	16.0	14.7	7.7	O1
3	28.0	34.2	10.1	
4	19.8	17.7	7.4	
5	22.9	15.1	7.1	
6	22.0	15.8	7.8	F4
7	22.6	17.1	7.7	
8	22.7	17.2	7.0	
9	17.6	12.7	7.0	F3
10	21.3	17.1	7.2	
SESSION AVG.	21.1	17.8	7.6	

TRIAL #	DELTA	28-40Hz	BETA	
1	10.3	4.1	6.1	
2	6.8	4.0	6.7	
3	9.7	4.3	6.5	
4	8.2	3.8	6.0	
5	7.0	4.4	6.6	
	LOW ALPHA	HIGH ALPHA	THETA	Fz
6	14.2	4.8	18.1	
7	13.3	5.3	21.9	
8	13.6	6.8	25.9	
9	12.2	7.3	23.8	
10	15.9	5.6	20.6	
SESSION AVG.	11.1	5.0	14.2	

Throughout this book we will be reviewing a great many data recordings of children with all manner of neurological issues that are adversely affecting their ability to pay attention and to learn. We will also be examining a great many records of children whose problems are emotional and behavioral in nature and not primarily the result of neurological problems. For the present purposes, I want to go through a basic data recording to illustrate

Figure 1.7   Summary statistics for the ClinicalQ shown in Figure 1.6. Areas of diagnostic importance are circled

	ClinicalQ Summary				
Cz	xϴ/β Rϴ/β	α↑%	α↓%	TA	
	2.70 3.09	30.0	1.3	43.3	
O1	α↑%	α↓%	EO	EC	
	99.6	20.4	2.08	2.77	
	ϴ/β	ϴ/α			
F4	2.94	1.43			
F3	3.04	1.24			
F=F%	β	α	ϴ		
	10.0	8.2	6.1		
Fz	Dz	Hβ/β	Σ	L/H	ϴ/β
	8.2	0.63	10.6	2. 43	3.37

how profoundly accurate and sensible the ClinicalQ EEG method is, relative to the ubiquitous top-down methods. I will not be going over all 21 summary markers shown in Figure 1.7, but just the essentials that guided me to a precise diagnosis of this problem. I will identify the specific items that facilitated the precision of diagnosis. Let's call them "red flags" and they are circled to set them apart from the other summary statistics.

As we proceed through the book looking at a number of different cases, the significance of these summary numbers will become apparent. For the present purposes, we want to focus only on those that have been circled to demonstrate the remarkable efficiency of allowing the brain to tell us what the problems are and where to go to fix them. The first red flags are at location Cz, directly on top of the head. The first number, 2.70, is the ratio of the amplitude of Theta (brain waves from 3–7 cycles per second) divided by the amplitude of Beta (brain waves from 16–25 cycles per second).

The Theta/Beta ratio is extremely important in that it gives us an indication of the level of arousal of specific areas of the brain. The American Academy of Neurology in a 2014 Evidence-Based Practice Advisory: *The utility of EEG theta/beta power ratio in the diagnosis of ADHD (DRAFT)*, (www.aan.com) indicted that the Theta/Beta ratio correctly identified 86.6 percent of patients clinically diagnosed with ADHD. The *Advisory* recommended that this ratio not be used in place of standard clinical evaluation because of risk of misdiagnosis of up to 15 percent of patients. We will see later in this book how more thorough assessment based on clinical database norms brings the "correct" diagnosis statistics remarkably close to 100 percent.

We have databases for clinical normative values for the normal functioning brain. The Theta/Beta ratio at that location for a child of about 14 years of age should be below about 2.20. Mitch's ratio was 2.70. What this tells us is that this child has some difficulty associated with focus. When that area of the brain is hypoactive as indicated by elevated Theta/Beta ratio, there is too much slow activity and/or too little fast activity. This indicates that Mitch is facing a challenge in terms of focus, concentration, attention, and staying on target. If that ratio was considerably greater, up in the range of four or so, we would likely be probing to determine if Mitch was hyperactive. However, in Mitch's case, it is more likely that his ADHD is of the inattentive variety.

What is most critical in this particular profile is the second number on that same line, which is 3.09. This is the Theta/Beta ratio that was obtained when the child was under cognitive challenge. This was done during the time that he was asked to read aloud. Notice that the number increased from 2.70 to 3.09. This is a particularly pernicious form of ADHD. When under cognitive challenge such as reading, the brain should be producing less slow frequency (that is, lower amplitude or strength) associated with hypoactivity, and/or greater fast activity associated with focus and attention. When it goes the opposite way (the ratio of the amplitude of slow frequency vs. high frequency gets larger), then this is a condition in which the harder the child tries, the worse the situation gets. We tend to find this condition mostly in males. The curious feature of this form of ADHD is that in some clients there are conditions in which the brain looks absolutely fine. The only time one sees the anomalous brain wave activity is when the child is being cognitively challenged. Thus, measuring brain wave activity when the child is simply sitting and not engaged does not reveal the condition that is causing the problems. Only when the child is asked to read aloud, or to count, do we see the elevated slow frequency amplitude.

The person who discovered this form of ADD was Professor George Fitzsimmons of the University of Alberta, Canada. The number of children who show the pattern just described (only see ADHD EEG profiles when being cognitively challenged) is not large. In most cases, one also sees neurological ADHD patterns even when the child is at rest. The important feature of this condition, however, is that cognitive challenge intensifies the condition. The usual result of this is that the harder the child tries, the worse the situation becomes. When trying to concentrate, the brain is showing greater amplitude of a brain wave that is associated with daydreaming and early stages of sleep! The tragic result is that children like this are highly at risk for simply giving up! They make determined efforts to keep up, and despite these efforts, they fall behind. These kids conclude that they are stupid or deficient in some way and simply give up. The giving up may have the form of rebellion, aggressive behavior, defiance and the like, or simply withdrawal. And our prisons are overloaded with the casualties of this condition. We will review some of the consequences of untreated ADHD in adult populations in the next chapter.

Now, returning to the clinical summary, we see the Theta/Beta ratios are 2.94 at F4, which is the right frontal cortex, and 3.04 at F3, which is the left frontal cortex. Whenever we see elevated slow frequency or elevated Theta/Beta ratio over the sensory motor cortex (that is, location Cz), we typically see it as well in the frontal cortex. Elevated Theta/Beta ratio in the frontal cortex is associated with hypoactivity of these regions of the brain and reflected in some inefficiency in cognitive processing.

So, the first thing I know about this child is that he has a pernicious form of ADHD. In general, I know that the child has likely made efforts to try to pay attention and do his homework. However, he finds that no matter how hard he tries, the problems simply seem to get worse. There are several other flags in Mitch's ClinicalQ that we will attend to shortly but at this point I have enough information from the three circled areas (CZ, F3, and F4) to be able to discuss the situation with the child in front of me. So I say to, Mitch, "Mitch what the brain is telling me is that you have some problems staying focused in class. You find it difficult to pay attention, your mind tends to wander and you have the same kind of problem when you try to do homework."

I now have Mitch's attention—he's focused on me. "But there is another thing in this record," I continue, "that's really problematic. And it always causes students a lot of difficulty. What the brain is telling me is that the harder you try the worse the situation gets. No matter how hard you try, most of the time you find it extremely difficult to stay focused and on target both in class and when you are trying to do homework. This is a problem we find mostly in men and it really makes you want to just give up!"

As is common at this point in my feedback to the child, Mitch is having difficulty maintaining composure. As I have been told by many children after their treatment is completed they found that I was the "one person on the planet who understood" (to quote one recent client) what the situation was. They did not have to spend any time telling me what the problem was—I was able to see it from what the brain was telling me.

At this point I turned to Mitch's mother and asked if she would mind if I spoke with Mitch privately for a few moments. I often do this with teenage male clients for I find that it provides an opportunity for getting the child on board and committed to therapy. This is an opportunity to speak with the child without parents interrupting by making comments and preventing me from developing good clinical attachment and report with the child.

In this particular case I noted several features of Mitch's brain assessment that made me suspicious about marijuana use. These indicators were elevated slow frequency Alpha and elevated slow frequency in the back the brain under eyes closed conditions. Very often you find this with individuals who are cannabis users. I decided to take a chance once I had developed some rapport with Mitch. Mitch and I spoke further about the use of neurotherapy with professional athletes. I then said: "Mitch it is important that you be part of your treatment team. I can help you with the brain inefficiencies that I see here in this brain map but it's important that you do what is necessary for these treatments to be really effective. And what I want you to do is stop smoking dope. Don't say 'yes' or 'no.' If you're not smoking dope so much the better but I'm getting some markers in your brain map that are often associated with cannabis use. If you are, stop because it makes people stupid. What cannabis does is it slows down a really important waveform in the brain and we certainly don't want that to happen."

As it turns out I was correct. Mitch was experimenting with marijuana. Mitch was so shaken by the accuracy of the brain wave assessment that I think he was shocked into stopping the marijuana use on-the-spot. We had a number of conversations and he shared with me later that he really felt like just quitting. He tearfully related that no matter how hard he tried, he simply could not function efficiently in school. He had great difficulty staying on target, doing his homework, and not "looking stupid." He said he just couldn't wait until he could stop going to school. Neurotherapy saved this child's life, a sentiment expressed on several occasions by his mother.

This is the form of ADHD that, in my judgment, is the one form that is most represented in the statistics associated with ADHD and criminality. These are the kids that quit; these are the kids that become truant; these are the kids that act up in school; these are the kids that become marginalized; these are the kids that get themselves into trouble; and these are the kids that are associated with the statistics about the number of incarcerated youth that have the symptoms of ADHD.

So the 14-year-old lad who came into my office in a sullen, bored, and clearly frightened state was indeed fortunate because the diagnosis and treatment of this child at this age clearly saved his life. Looking at the risk factors, it only makes sense to neurologically evaluate the condition of these children as soon as they run into difficulty in school. Teachers and parents are very aware of these behaviors very early in the child's life. The ease with which we can assess and diagnose the neurological anomalies is such that it is a tragedy that we are not doing so in our school systems. Not only would it save the child's life but it would save taxpayers a fortune!

Mitch, by the way, is going on 20 at the time of this writing and is in the first few weeks of the third-year of his undergraduate studies. Mitch had a total of 33 sessions between the ages of 14 and 16 and came back for a few more treatments about two years ago when he felt that he was struggling at university. Mitch still feels that he struggles more than other students at university, although one wouldn't know it by his grades. He proudly reported that he has nothing below the grade of B+!

TWO

The Attention Deficit
Hyperactivity Disorders

In this chapter, the focus is on the disorders that are, indeed, disorders of attention. In this category are neurological conditions that directly affect attention and hyperactivity. These are situations in which the symptoms are not primarily the result of some other condition such as depression. Much has been written about various forms of ADHD and yet we find that there is no consensus on these forms among researchers and clinicians. Most of these variations in forms of ADHD are really ADHD plus various comorbid conditions such as sleep disturbance, depression, oppositional behavior, anxiety, and the like. As the reader will find, the labels and types of ADHD are largely irrelevant. From the perspective of bottom-up we look at the neurology of the child and correct relevant anomalies in functioning.

In later chapters, the conditions that interfere with a child's ability to be attentive in school but are not neurological disorders of attention are reviewed. These will include conditions of poor stress tolerance, predisposition to depression, oppositional and defiance disorders, and frightened and traumatized children.

One of the problems we have with the statistics associated with consequences of untreated ADHD is that the methods for diagnosing these conditions are so flawed. As pointed out earlier, the top-down method for diagnosis of attention deficiencies is simply inappropriate. However, with this in mind, let us remember some of the sequellae of untreated attention problems.

There is disagreement among researchers about the risk factors associated with untreated ADHD. Part of this problem, of course, is the fact that ADHD is a "wastebasket diagnosis." However, most of the disagreement is not about the fact that untreated ADHD leads to life complications; rather, that this disagreement centers on the extent of the risk. And as we shall review at various times throughout this book, different forms of ADHD pose different risks for individuals who remain untreated into adulthood. Other factors, of course, are important, including any psychological comorbidity one might have such as depression and anxiety, as well as gender and culture, to name but a few.

Although there are some inconsistencies in the data, nonetheless a relationship between untreated ADHD and criminality seems clear. Data collected on incarcerated males (research by Michael Rosler and colleagues published in 2003 in *European Archieves in Psychiatry*) indicate much higher proportions of those with ADHD-like behaviors than in the general population. Interestingly, these individuals are not only more likely to be charged with a crime and arrested, but they are also more likely to be indicted, and far more likely to be imprisoned. Perhaps this simply indicates again that they lack the capability for responsible planning, organizing, sequencing, and monitoring of their personal situation once they have been charged with a crime, as has been suggested in a review article by Dr. Christine Low in the February 2015 issue of the *Brown University Child and Adolescent Behavior Letter*).

A recent study by Dr. Ylva Ginsberg and colleagues (2012) of long-term male inmates in a Swedish prison found that 40 percent had ADHD and less than 7 percent of that group had ever been diagnosed with this condition. Another recent study by Drs. Jason Fletcher and Barbara Wolfe (2009) of Yale University of 13,000 adolescents over a long time period found that those with ADHD were twice as likely to commit a robbery and 50 percent more likely to have sold drugs, as compared to their peers.

So, it seems clear that undiagnosed and untreated ADHD is a very substantial risk factor for criminal and otherwise irresponsible behavior. The challenge is to make sure that we treat the behaviors that are causing the trouble and not be corralled by the label we put on a specified grouping of these troublesome behaviors. Doing the latter markedly reduces our success rate for helping children overcome these hurdles to successful and fulfilling lives. And we should remember that ADHD may start in childhood but it persists into adulthood in about half of the affected individuals. The data shown in Table 2.1 come from various studies of risk factors associated with ADHD. And although one can quibble about the magnitude of some of these findings, nonetheless the data are striking. The table summarizes statistics from various studies of the consequences of untreated ADHD. The data include adult populations of individuals whose ADHD was either not diagnosed properly and/or did not receive proper and efficient treatment for the condition.

Table 2.1   ADHD Associated Risks

Adults

About 50 percent co-morbidity with depression and anxiety disorders

Source: Kaplan (2012).

ADHD is five to ten times more common among adult alcoholics

Source: Smith (2002).

Children

About 40 percent co-morbidity with depression
Between 20 and 40 percent co-morbidity with anxiety disorders
Four times greater risk of drug abuse disorders
Increased risk for suicide attempts

Source: Faraone & Kunwar, Medscape Psychiatry.

Criminal behavior

Twice as likely to have been arrested
Three times more likely to be convicted for a criminal offense
Fifteen times higher incarceration rate

Source: Mannuzza et al. (2008).

Comorbid mood and anxiety disorders are very common with ADHD. This is not surprising considering the effects of untreated ADHD on adults. Many of these individuals have difficulty staying in school and/or training programs, sustaining relationships, and sustaining employment. They have problems with planning, organizing, sequencing, and following through on tasks. Many of the clients we see who live with ADHD that was untreated are in states of what we might call reactive depression or despair. Life is just not going well for them. Often they have been in multiple relationships and things are not going well in their present relationship. This is often directly related to their inability to plan ahead and organize their lives. In addition, they usually have difficulty handling finances properly and trouble with participating in an organized and emotionally functional and rational relationship.

Hence, these people frequently come for treatment complaining of depression when, in fact, it is reactive depression; they are depressed because of their life circumstances not because of any neurological predisposition to depressed mood states. They have one of the ADHD conditions! Although, of course, they may have neurologically based depression as well.

These people are often extremely anxious as well. They may be in serious financial difficulty because of the ADHD affecting their careers and affecting their ability to manage finances properly. We certainly see very high levels of comorbidity at the Swingle Clinic. And we see both sides of this dimension: people who come in with a diagnosis of depression who are depressed because of the effects of ADHD, and alternatively, people who come in with a diagnosis of ADHD who are depressed with symptoms of lack of interest, poor motivation, and fatigue. The significant diagnostic precision of the ClinicalQ allows us to accurately isolate the areas of the brain causing the problems. We can then, in turn, develop neurotherapy treatment protocols that efficiently treat these conditions. The label for the pathology is obviously of trivial importance.

THE CHATTERING BRAIN

The data associated with risk of alcoholism and other addictions is not as clear-cut. Certainly, depression and anxiety, as just described, might well lead to self-medicating behavior in which the person drinks to get some peace and forget his or her troubles. However, it could be a neurological condition associated with genetic predisposition to hyper-arousal that is strongly related to vulnerability to alcoholism. This neurological predisposition turns up routinely in children and adults diagnosed with ADHD. Neurologically, this condition is indicated by a marked deficiency in the ratio of the strength of slow frequency (Theta) divided by the strength of fast frequency (Beta) brain wave activity in the back of the brain.

People with this condition in the back of the brain report that they have difficulty quieting themselves. They simply cannot find a switch to turn the brain off. People with this neurological pattern complain of poor stress tolerance, predisposition to anxiety, self-medicating behavior, sleep quality problems, chatter in the head, and fatigue. The deficient Theta/Beta ratio can be associated with either a deficiency in Theta amplitude or an excess of Beta amplitude, and sometimes both. As discussed in Chapter One, the precision of the ClinicalQ initial EEG assessment provides precise data on the brain wave activity. Thus, we know if we need to increase Theta amplitude, decrease

Beta amplitude, or both, to effectively and efficiently treat this condition. It is interesting to note that the symptoms associated with the deficient Theta/Beta ratio in the occipital region are often quite different depending on whether the deficiency is related to excessive Beta or deficient Theta amplitude. The brain location implicated in this condition is shown in Figure 2.1.

Figure 2.1   Deficient Theta/Beta Ratio

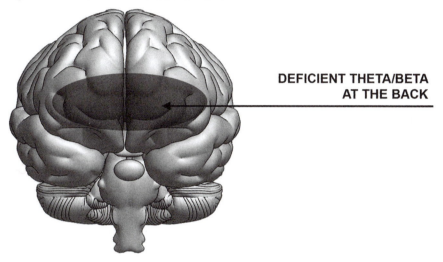

DEFICIENT THETA/BETA
AT THE BACK

Children with this condition are routinely diagnosed with ADHD. And, as we have just discussed, in reality, this is a form of genetic predisposition to addictive behavior found in children diagnosed with an attention problem prior to any exposure to alcohol or other substances. In adult populations with this form of attention problem, we find the expected elevated levels of alcoholism and other substance addictions, including nicotine.

The child with this condition simply cannot sit still, experiences disconcerting brain chatter, has poor tolerance to stress, often has poor sleep quality, is very easily distracted, and often does not do well in school. Although diagnosed with ADHD because of poor focus, easy distractibility, and elevated activity levels, medicating this child with a stimulant may exacerbate the problem. Hence, although we prefer to treat this condition with neurotherapy without medications, nonetheless we consult with physicians for clients who prefer medication. In this condition, stimulants are contraindicated and alternative medications would be recommended.

THE HYPOACTIVE BRAIN (INATTENTIVE)

Recognizing that there are many reasons why children cannot pay attention in school, many of which we will review in later chapters, we will start with a review of those neurological conditions that directly affect the child's ability to pay attention in school. Related to these conditions are conditions that are also associated with hyperactivity. In many circumstances, the brain wave pattern associated with an attention problem is also the one associated with the hyperactivity issue.

We start with what I call Common Attention Deficit Disorder (CADD). This is the least complicated form of an attention deficit disorder and the most easily corrected. As shown in Figure 2.2, CADD is associated with elevated slow frequency amplitude. Frequencies in the Theta range (3–7 Hz) are elevated, typically over the center and frontal regions of the brain but, as shown in the figure, often over the entire cortex. When slow frequency is elevated in the brain it means that those areas are hypoactive. These are the children who daydream a lot, simply cannot stay focused, are disorganized, and have very great difficulty staying on target.

Figure 2.2   Topograph of child with elevated Theta amplitude

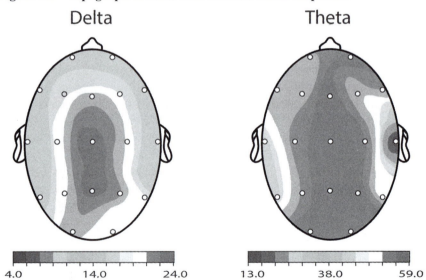

In the best of all possible worlds, we see these children at a very young age. As I say in my workshops, a client directly from heaven is a little girl, perhaps eight years of age, who has this simple form of CADD. Most importantly, she knows from the depth of her heart that the love of her parents for her is completely independent of any achievements she may attain. I can bet the farm that this child will respond very successfully to treatment and that treatment will likely only require between 15 and 20 sessions.

Just such a child is shown in Figure 2.3. The initial data recorded at the intake assessment is shown on the top and labeled baseline. As you will note, the Theta/Beta ratio (the ratio of the amplitude of 3–7 Hz divided by the amplitude of 16–25 Hz) is 3.5. Anything above about 2.3 or so, with a child of her age, is usually indicative of an inattention issue. We would consider that this condition is of moderate severity.

Figure 2.3   Intake and treatment progress of child with CADD

	THETA	BETA	THETA/BETA @ Cz
BASELINE	21.9	6.3	3.5
TREATMENTS			
1	20.7	5.1	4.0
2	17.0	4.9	3.5
3	21.1	5.2	4.0
4	21.1	5.4	3.9
5	22.5	5.3	5.2
6	23.1	5.3	4.4
7	22.3	5.2	4.3
8	26.4	5.7	4.6
9	22.5	5.8	3.9
10	23.8	5.9	4.0
11	23.4	5.8	4.0
12	21.2	5.1	4.2
13	23.7	5.7	4.2
14	22.5	5.1	4.4
15	17.5	4.5	3.9
16	12.6	5.0	2.5
17	10.6	7.8	1.4
18	10.8	7.9	1.4
19	10.9	7.4	1.5
20	10.6	7.6	1.4

The treatment for this is very straightforward. As described in Chapter Six, the child is engaged in a video game that she plays with her brain. When the brain is doing what we want it to do, icons move on the computer screen and this can be any one of a number of different games that are used for neuronal feedback. Note that in the initial sessions the Theta/Beta ratio appears to be getting worse. She started at 3.5 but during the first 15 or so sessions the ratio appears to be getting larger. It is not unusual that during the initial sessions the ratio appears to be getting worse. This may be related to the form of ADHD we reviewed in Chapter One of the boy whose ratio became worse under challenge. Recall that the initial value shown on the baseline is an average value. When this child makes considerable effort during the treatment then the ADHD condition worsens in many cases. It is very important for parents and the neurotherapist to understand that very often you get an increase in the symptom prior to symptom improvement. In the case of the young girl, when we were challenging the child, the condition continued to worsen until after 18 sessions when she finally got it! The Theta/Beta ratio dropped markedly at that point and was sustained for the final few sessions.

Figure 2.4 is a letter sent by the parents of this child. The important matter to note here is that the mother points out that the child, after a week of school, brought in her flute and played a solo in front of her classmates. It is also

Figure 2.4   Mother's letter regarding effects of neurotherapy for her daughter

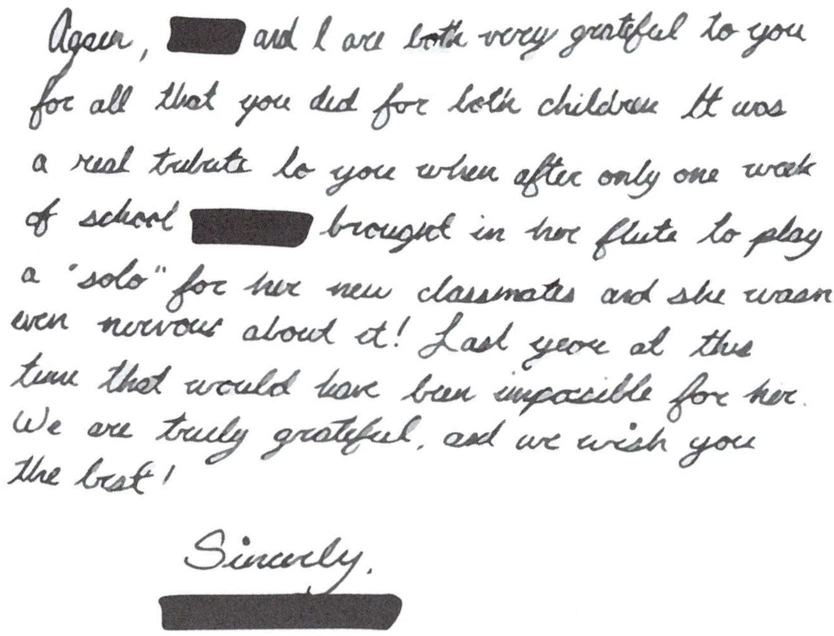

interesting to note that this child changed schools so this was a completely new environment for her and none of the classmates were familiar to her. But as the mother points out, she was not the least bit nervous, whereas in the previous year, before her treatment, it would have been impossible for her to perform in front of her classmates.

It is important to note that when you successfully treat ADHD, you also are treating the child's self-esteem. Children who have attention problems are very concerned about their performance. They see their classmates progressing in school with apparently much less difficulty than they are having. They question their intelligence, and they question their self-worth. Regrettably, if parents are not supportive, understanding, and helpful, but are instead judgmental, then the child's self-esteem suffers an even more severe blow. Once the ADHD was corrected, self-esteem was improved and she was able to perform her solo performance. As the saying goes "fix the child's self-esteem and you fix everything."

THE HYPOACTIVE BRAIN (HYPERACTIVITY)

The difference between the inattentive and the hyperactive forms of ADHD is associated with two neurological factors. The first factor is a matter of degree. Common ADD is associated with elevated amplitude of slow frequency brain wave activity primarily measured over the central part of the brain, but in general, spreads out over most of the cortex. This is shown in the topographical maps of Figure 2.2 in which Theta amplitude is seen to be elevated over the entire brain. At lower levels of elevated slow frequency, one gets inattentive forms of ADD. These are the children that simply cannot stay focused and are easily distracted and prone to daydreaming, just like our little eight-year-old girl described earlier. At higher levels of excessive slow frequency amplitude, the brain is seriously hypoactive and the child desperately needs stimulation. The hyperactivity is best conceptualized as self-medicating behavior. It is hard for us to appreciate the fact that sitting still is painful for the child. The movement activates brain activity principally over the sensory motor cortex, thus relieving the feelings of discomfort for the child. The primary areas associated with this elevated slow frequency are the central regions over the sensory motor cortex.

Occasionally, we have a complicating factor, such as a deficiency of slow frequency in the back of the brain. Deficiency of slow frequency amplitude in the back of the brain is associated with poor stress tolerance, anxiety, and difficulty sitting still. If we are only dealing with the issue of elevated slow frequency over the sensory motor cortex (the area directly on top of the head in Figure 2.5), then stimulant drugs such as methylphenidate can be helpful because the drug stimulates the brain; hence, the child's need to self-medicate with hyperactivity is minimized. If, however, we have the complicating factor of a deficiency of slow frequency amplitude, or elevated fast frequency amplitude in the back of the brain (i.e., low Theta/Beta ratio), then often drugs that are central nervous system stimulants, like methylphenidate, can exacerbate the problem.

Figure 2.5   Brain regions associated with hyperactive forms of ADHD

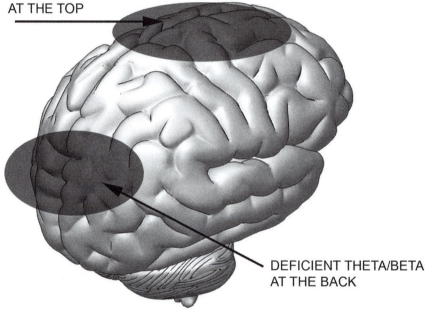

TOO MUCH THETA
AT THE TOP

DEFICIENT THETA/BETA
AT THE BACK

The neurotherapeutic treatment of this condition is identical to the treatment of the less severe inattentive form. Basically, we decrease slow frequency amplitude and/or increase the faster frequencies over the sensory motor cortex (top of the head). The difference in treatment procedures for the "inattentive" ADHD child as opposed to the "hyperactive" ADHD child can be more than just a matter of degree. Again, depending on the age at which the child commences treatment, the ADHD child with the strong hyperactive component can be more of a behavioral problem in school and is likely being reinforced for highly disruptive behavior. This scenario sets up a pattern of reinforcing disruptive behavior with disciplinary actions, such as sending the child the principal's office, having the child go out in the hallway, or forcing the child to sit in an isolated corner of the classroom. A very sensible alternative to this procedure is the "safe room." which is discussed in Chapter Five. For the present discussion, we want to keep in mind that the principal difference between the hyperactive and the purely inattentive ADHD child is more than simply a matter of degree. Because of the hyperactivity component, the child is likely to develop secondary problems, such as those just mentioned, because the child is being reinforced with significant attention for highly disruptive behavior.

HIGH FRONTAL ALPHA ADHD

Too much Alpha in the front part of the brain can be a serious problem. We find this condition with many clients coming to the Swingle Clinic with diagnoses such as bipolar disorder, major depression, or the personality disorders. Cognitively, clients with high frontal Alpha forms of ADHD complain of problems with planning, organizing, sequencing, and following through on things. At the emotional level, individuals with high frontal Alpha also complain of problems with emotional flightiness, hyper-verbosity, and problems with emotional volatility, grounding, and consistency.

It is also interesting to note that this is one of the conditions in which, historically, there has been discrimination against females in that male children received therapeutic attention more readily and systematically than females. The reason for this is that the female child with this condition was likely to be viewed as highly social, chatty, and flighty, but not too bright. The high frontal Alpha ADHD went undiagnosed because these behaviors and mood states were consistent with cultural negative stereotypes of female behavior. If diagnosed and treated properly at a young age, the lives of these children are literally saved.

Many adult females with this high frontal Alpha condition come to our clinic with their lives in shambles. Their relationships have not progressed adequately. They report having problems at all levels of their schooling, often dropping out prior to program completion. They have been unable to achieve their career aspirations. They feel emotionally unstable. The reason for their distress is pretty straightforward: these are the consequences associated with the high frontal Alpha form of ADHD concomitant with the emotional and cognitive dysregulation characteristics of this condition. The brain area associated with the high frontal Alpha form of ADHD is shown in Figure 2.6. As the topograph shows, the elevated Alpha is most pronounced in the frontal brain regions. Figure 2.6 shows the topograph output from an

EEG of an actual client with a severe high frontal Alpha ADHD condition. Alpha, for this client, is elevated over the entire cortex but most prominently over the frontal cortex.

Figure 2.6   Topograph showing distribution of Alpha brain wave amplitude of a client with high frontal Alpha ADHD

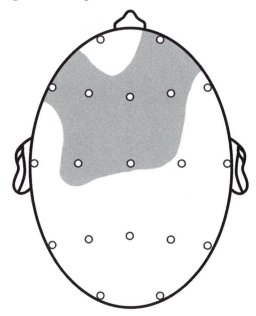

Alpha is like a parking frequency in the brain. Too much Alpha in the area of the brain associated with cognitive and emotional regulation results in these areas being hypoactive and, hence, cognitive and emotional dysregulation occurs. High frontal Alpha becomes even more problematic when the person has other neurological predispositions for problematic conditions. These predispositions can include depression, poor stress tolerance, and perseverative thought processes. It is not difficult to understand how the Alpha dysregulation of emotional and cognitive functioning, when combined with predisposition to depression, poor stress, tolerance or anxiety, would be associated with diagnoses such as bipolar disorder or agitated depression.

Even without these other compounding conditions, individuals can be seen as emotionally unstable because of the emotional dysregulation factor.

Frontal Alpha emotional dysregulation often results in individuals going in and out of depressed and/or agitated mood states. Combined with the cognitive dysregulation, these individuals have difficulty sustaining focus and problems with planning, organizing, sequencing, and following through on tasks. These combinations of emotional and cognitive difficulties give rise to substantial difficulties in school, work, social, and intimate relationship situations.

It is easy to imagine how the emotional dysregulation, often associated with chattiness, further gives rise to difficulties these children experience in school. They have trouble staying seated. They are always bouncing around, socializing with other children, and causing significant disruption in the classroom. These are the children who will be talking to other children when they are supposed to be attending to the teacher. They have very great difficulty sustaining attention. What follows is an example of one such case.

Figure 2.7 provides a summary of the intake ClinicalQ of a young woman with high frontal Alpha form of ADHD. The elevated frontal Alpha of this client is similar to that shown in the topographical representation of the client shown in Figure 2.6. The data indicate that there are no significant inefficiencies in brain functioning other than a marked elevation of Alpha amplitude at locations F3 and F4, the frontal cortex. This is shown on the lines of data associated with F4 and F3. The ratio of Theta to Alpha is 0.54

Figure 2.7   Data summary of EEG of a client with high frontal Alpha form of ADHD

Cz	$x\Theta/\beta$	$R\Theta/\beta$	$\alpha\uparrow\%$	$\alpha\downarrow\%$	TA		
	2.08	2.00	43.6	12.3	26.9		
O1	$\alpha\uparrow\%$	$\alpha\downarrow\%$	EO	EC			
	112.6	22.6	1.67	1.52			
	β	α	Θ		Θ/β	Θ/α	
F4	7.9	14.4	6.2		1.27	0.54	
F3	7.2	13.7	5.9		1.24	0.52	
F=F%	β	α	Θ				
	5.1	5.1	9.7				
Fz	Dz	$H\beta/\beta$	Σ	L/H			
	5.7	0.58	12.5	0.67			

at location F4 and 0.52 at location F3. The ratios should be closer to 1.50, or so, in each location; that is, the amount of Theta (amplitude of brain waves between 3–7 Hz) should be about 50 percent greater than the amplitude of Alpha (8–12 Hz). This can also be seen in the amplitudes shown in lines F4 and F3. The Alpha amplitude is 14.4, almost twice the amplitude of Theta (7.9) and similarly, at F3, the Alpha is 13.7 and the Theta is only 7.2 (these amplitudes are in microvolts).

When this young woman presented for treatment, let's call her Jane, she seemed depressed and agitated. She started to cry when she was describing how she felt her life was in chaos. She had just left a relationship that had been ongoing for about three years, and was in a job she considered boring and well-below her level of capability. She just felt rotten. She had gone to see her physician on a number of occasions trying to describe her condition. Her physician felt that she was depressed and had prescribed antidepressants. In a condition such as this, antidepressants are obviously ineffective, short of sedation levels.

Jane, like many clients, was profoundly relieved to see that there was, in fact, a neurological reason for her chaotic, unfulfilled, and unfulfilling life. She went on to describe her early life in school in which her most profound memory was one of struggling to keep up. Everyone thought she was very sweet and nice but she clearly remembered feeling as though she was stupid. She simply could not keep up with the other children. Her parents were very supportive and patient and provided her with tutors to help her get through her homework. She just was not able to stay focused; she was not able to plan and organize her daily activities. A poignant memory she related was of her going to her music lesson, having forgotten to bring her musical instrument and feeling absolutely humiliated.

There were many such experiences that Jane related during the initial visit. She concluded by stating that her early childhood was simply miserable and it was miserable not because her family was not supportive and loving, but simply because she could not function properly in the school environment. The tragedy here is that a lot of this could have been prevented if she had been properly diagnosed at a young age. A simple six-minute brain assessment would have identified the problem and a few very straightforward treatment procedures would have just simply changed her life.

It is a truism, of course, that the older we get, the longer it takes for the body and the mind to heal or to change. It is no different with neurotherapy. Treatment of an eight-year-old with Jane's condition would likely be resolvable in 15 to 25 sessions, whereas with Jane, more sessions were likely to be required. However, in addition to the possibility of a less plastic brain, there are other issues associated with dealing with older patients. The longer this condition has continued, the more failed relationships, the more failed jobs, and the more broken and shattered dreams. So in addition to the neurology, we have all of the psychological baggage that is associated with this form of ADHD: failure after failure after failure. If a client can really embrace the metaphor: "look out the windshield, not the rear-view mirror" then, of course, far fewer sessions are required to deal with the psychological aspect of this ADHD situation.

Jane was very fortunate she had a very high IQ. This is indicated by the very low ratio of slow to fast Alpha on the summary sheet (0.67—anything below 1.50 is okay!). In addition, her brain functioning was quite within normal limits in all other areas with the exception of the high frontal Alpha. In short, we did not have a lot of other things that had to be corrected.

Jane finished her therapy in 22 sessions. She registered for a few courses to gain experience and regain her confidence at being able to do academic work. She got started on changing her life. This process took the better part of three years in which she got herself trained to pursue her dream of becoming a nurse. We saw Jane for follow-up visits four times during that three-year period just to make sure that all of the neurological gains she had made remained stable. She felt that additional psychotherapy was not required, a sentiment with which I was in complete agreement.

Jane was lucky. She had a loving and caring family. She was very bright. The carnage associated with her high Alpha form of ADHD was not so overwhelming that she was not able to dig herself out and get on with her life once the neurological condition had been corrected. Although I do not have two cents worth of evidence to support this, my suspicion is that the reason she made out so well is because of the firm, loving, and structured family environment she had during the early years when she was suffering in school. Her core emotional belief about herself was not irrevocably destroyed by a sense of worthlessness. Jane was also very lucky in that other than the high frontal Alpha ADHD, she had no other significant brain wave inefficiencies. Many people are not as lucky as Jane.

AN ADULT WITH CADD

As in all areas of endeavor, some things are easy and some things are difficult. In neurotherapy, as I like to say, some clients come directly from heaven and some clients come from hell. The little girl whom we discussed earlier, the eight-year-old with CADD and loving and supportive parents, came directly from heaven. Clients who come from other areas vary, but one in particular that has a high likelihood of coming from someplace other than heaven is the adult male with untreated ADHD. And a major reason that these clients are difficult is not because of the neurology.

Figure 2.8   An adult male with CADD

Cz	$x\Theta/\beta$	$R\Theta/\beta$	$\alpha\uparrow\%$	$\alpha\downarrow\%$	TA
	3.28	3.05	75.1	17.2	48.7

O1	$\alpha\uparrow\%$	$\alpha\downarrow\%$	EO	EC
	178.0	12.3	2.82	1.95

	β	α	Θ	Θ/β	Θ/α
F4	26.7	19.9	9.1	2.93	1.34
F3	25.4	16.5	8.3	3.06	1.54

F=F%	β	α	Θ
	9.6	20.6	5.1

Fz	Dz	$H\beta/\beta$	Σ	L/H
	15.2	0.57	13.2	1.48

In Figure 2.8, we show the summary of the initial intake ClinicalQ for a 35-year-old male, let us call him Bruce, with CADD. As you can see, there is nothing extraordinary about this EEG profile. Bruce has CADD just like the little girl we discussed earlier and the numbers are not quite as severe as in her case. What makes this condition difficult, or potentially difficult, is what I call "psychological baggage." Adult males with ADHD often come reluctantly into my office, having been referred by a parent, relative, or spouse. Probably more accurately, they have been dragged in by their ear! They are not happy to be in my office, which is quite apparent from their demeanor. They slouch in the chair and try to be affable and marginally interested. After a bit of chit chat, they state that they are just interested in seeing what this is all about. When describing their condition, they state that they are "just a laid back, easygoing, disorganized kind of guy that other people get all uptight about."

Typically at this point in the session I look the client in the eye and say "You don't believe that for a moment! My guess is that you're having or have had difficulty in school; you have difficulty holding down a job; feel that your career dream is unattainable; have difficulty in your intimate relationships. And deep down in the quiet of the night you have frightening feelings of inadequacy."

Depending upon the reaction I get, I may go on about this a bit longer but in general what I am trying to do is point out to this type of client that we are not going to play his game. I am also quite straightforward with him that the neurology is easy; dealing with his psychological baggage is what is going to be the difficult problem. He has incorporated his attention deficit problem into his definition of his personality (i.e., "I am just an easy going, laid back, disorganized kind of guy"). Overcoming this defense to inadequacy is going to be the major challenge.

Let us look at the summary data for Bruce. What we see is the Theta/Beta ratio on top of the head is 3.28, which is quite a bit above the maximum of 2.2 or so that we would expect for his age. The good news is that under cognitive challenge the Theta/Beta ratio drops (to 3.05). This is quite different from the brain wave data of Mitch that we described in Chapter One. Recall, Mitch's Theta/Beta ratio became worse under cognitive challenge. Mitch's is a far more pernicious form of ADHD because what it does is negate the child's efforts to focus. The harder Mitch tried, the worse the situation became.

Although Bruce has a relatively high Theta/Beta ratio, nonetheless, he is not burdened with that added problem of cognitive activity making the ADHD worse. That part of the neurology news is positive in that elevated slow frequency brain wave amplitude forms of ADHD are relatively easy and straightforward to treat.

The second thing that we notice with Bruce is that the Delta amplitude is elevated as well. The Delta is 15.2 in the front and it should be below 10. The Theta/Beta ratios are approximately 3 at both the right and left side of the front part of the brain and 3.28 over the sensory motor strip (location Cz). You will also note that there is an imbalance in Alpha amplitude in the front part of the brain, where the right is 20.8 percent greater in amplitude relative to the left. If this were a young 10-year-old boy, I would be asking his mother about oppositional and defiant forms of behavior. This Alpha imbalance is a marker for oppositional/defiance behavior and in an adult male it is often a marker for an individual who has had substantial difficulties in terms of maintaining positive interpersonal relationships.

I often wonder about this imbalance in Alpha between the right and the left frontal cortex with the adult client. It is unusual to have clients with this imbalance not admit to some relationship problem with their spouse or intimate associate. In the young child, we see this expressed as oppositional and defiant behaviors. In the adult, I find this frequently with clients involved in nasty divorces and breakups. The question, of course, is: Does this imbalance reflect the angst of the breakup or is the breakup the result of the oppositional/defiant character of the client? It appears that this imbalance in Alpha amplitude between the right and the left prefrontal cortex regions can be reflective of a present interpersonal conflict or of an oppositional/defiant behavioral predisposition.

In the present situation, I simply pointed out to Bruce that this discrepancy is often associated with problems with opposition and defiance in young children, which often carries over into similar kinds of behaviors in the adult male. Irritability and aggressiveness are sometimes related to this disparity and with some difficulty getting along with people. Present experiences of some difficulties with interpersonal relationships are also often captured in the ClinicalQ reflected in the imbalances in Alpha amplitude, with the right frontal cortex being greater than the left. In the present case, Bruce admitted to having problems with opposition and defiance as a young child and he also admitted to difficulties with his present relationship.

Bruce's case brings up an interesting issue associated with doing bottom-up versus top-down assessment and therapy. Bruce came to my clinic for attention problems. The ClinicalQ brain assessment indicated that Bruce did indeed have a neurological condition associated with problems of attention. However, the brain EEG also indicated the frontal cortex dysfunction that is associated with interpersonal factors. Clients with the Alpha amplitude imbalances can have problems with oppositional or defiant behavior, irritability, "short fuse," or aggressiveness. It appears that this imbalance also reflects extant interpersonal problematic situations such as breakup of a relationship, problems with co-workers or superiors, bullying, or sexual harassment. Again, as in Bruce's case, we do not know if the extant interpersonal problems are caused by the neurological predisposition to socially agonistic attitudes and behavior or if the interpersonally problematic situation gives rise to the imbalance. We do know that both circumstances are found coincident with the Alpha imbalance and we have clinical data supporting each condition. In particular, we have a number of cases in which the Alpha imbalance appears in the EEG of clients already in treatment. Inevitably, when queried, these clients admit to a recent or present interpersonal crisis including situations such as breakdown of a relationship/marriage, bullying (with both children and adults), and severe sexual harassment in the workplace. As will be discussed in Chapter Four, the bullying EEG profile we see in school-age children typically includes both the Alpha imbalance and a marked blunting of the Alpha response indicative of emotional trauma.

At still another level of interpretation, it is completely reasonable to assume that Bruce's ADHD condition created situations that resulted in the interpersonal angst to which he admits. ADHD adult males simply cannot "get it together." They have problems with planning, organizing, and task completion so their finances, work situation, and interpersonal relationships are usually in some state of chronic chaos.

The complexity of the psychological baggage that accompanies Bruce's apparently simple ADHD reminds me to again emphasize to the reader, as I will be repeating frequently in this book, that neurotherapy is not a stand-alone treatment. You want to be treated by a LICENCED ("registered" in some jurisdictions) health care provider qualified to deal with these complexities. One-size-fits-all neurofeedback franchises simply are inadequate and potentially dangerous.

So, as the reader will note, although Bruce came to the Swingle Clinic for treatment of a concentration/attention problem, the ClinicalQ EEG revealed other psycho/social difficulties. Clients are usually quite startled by the precision of the ClinicalQ for identifying not only the extant condition that brought them to the clinic but also for identifying other conditions/situations impacting on their life. Bruce was no exception. He was very impressed with the accuracy of the interpretation. He agreed to pursue treatment and we had a few sessions focused on developing behavioral courses of action to get his life in order. Bruce was "kicked out" (successfully finished treatment) of the clinic after 21 sessions. Follow-up sessions at 3 and 12 months found him functioning satisfactorily and his EEG changes were stable. "You changed my life," according to Bruce.

As was the case with Bruce, once I have reviewed the results of the ClinicalQ with these defiant, sullen, oppositional, frightened, and angry young men, they are usually on board with the therapy. They are so struck by the accuracy of the brain assessment that many of their defenses drop. I have many of these folks point out that I "nailed them." I was able to tell them exactly what the symptoms were based on six minutes of recording time (as described in detail in Chapter Three). More importantly, they really have the feeling that I understand the challenges they face. They also conclude that neurotherapy is a no-nonsense, data-driven, aggressive, and precisely focused treatment. We are not going to be sitting around holding hands trying to make the client feel good and develop strategies for coping with the situation. The goals of therapy are clear: improve the neurological basis for the problem(s) and, if needed, engage relevant behavioral/psychological therapies to plan, organize, and sequence important life changes. The latter may include setting goals and action plans for changes in career/work, relationships, personal development, and life-fulfilling avocational activities.

Remember Mitch from Chapter One? Figure 2.9 shows the summary table of Mitch's ClinicalQ. Mitch, of course, is the young child who experienced challenge-related exacerbations of his attention deficit problem. The principal difference between Bruce and Mitch is that the Theta/Beta ratio on top of the head (location Cz) becomes worse under cognitive challenge for Mitch, but better for Bruce. As previously described, Mitch's is a very pernicious form of ADHD. However, also note that Mitch does not have any imbalances in the frontal cortex. There are no neurological predispositions to oppositional/defiant behavior and no predisposition for emotional volatility. However, Mitch was oppositional and defiant.

Figure 2.9   A male child with cognitive challenge exacerbated ADHD

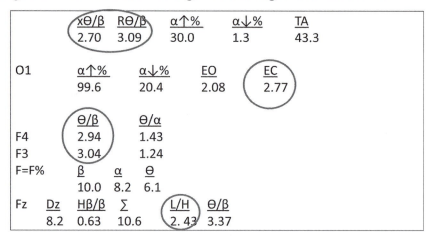

The difference between Bruce's and Mitch's ClinicalQs is a very good example of a situation in which opposition/defiance is primarily in response to feelings of failure in Mitch's case. There are no neurological predispositions to oppositional/defiant behavior in Mitch's brain assessment. Bruce, on the other hand, did have the discrepancy in Alpha in the front part of his brain that is the neurological predisposition for interpersonally agonistic attitudes. Again, it is important to note that a predisposition is simply that. When one is predisposed to something it does not necessarily mean that the situation is presently manifested. Something has to turn the key for a predisposition to become an actuality. Thus, it is important to keep in mind that behaviors can be associated with response to presently occurring situations or in response to a neurological predisposition. Frequently, of course, it is both in that a predisposition manifests and the manifestation of the predisposition triggers exacerbation in the condition associated with the neurological predisposition.

Figure 2.10 shows the data for Sam, a 40-year-old adult male with the pernicious form of ADHD, similar to the form that Mitch had. As shown in the figure, this is a pretty straightforward example of cognitive challenge activated ADHD. Under eyes open resting conditions, the Theta/Beta ratio is in an acceptable range of 2.1. However, when Sam started counting, the Theta amplitude increased by about 30 percent. In short, the brain was going the wrong way, increasing the strength of a brain wave that would be more appropriate for sleep or daydreaming, when he was trying to concentrate. Just like Mitch, Sam's recollection of his early childhood years is one of marked discouragement and despair. As hard as he tried, he simply could not keep up with the other children in his classes. Although he made out satisfactorily in school, Sam felt that he always had to put in strikingly more effort to achieve mediocre grades as compared with other children who, with far less effort, were achieving much higher grades.

Figure 2.10   An adult male with challenge exacerbated ADHD

		THETA/BETA @ Cz
EYES OPEN		2.1
COUNTING		2.8

		TREATMENT
WEEK	1	2.2
	3	1.7
	7	1.5
	9	1.5
	12	1.3

Sam learned a few tricks to help when he was trying to study or do cognitively challenging work. In high school, he studied with a radio on which, of course, drove his parents crazy. They believed, as most parents would, that Sam could not possibly study better with a radio on. But in fact, Sam was correct! The extra stimulation reduced the Theta amplitude and even though distracting, the radio made it somewhat easier for Sam to maintain focus. We might think of this as one salient distractor minimizing the impact of many lesser distractors in his brain.

The other trick Sam learned was to stand up while he was reading or trying to memorize something. This calls to mind a story I heard about Earnest Hemingway who apparently also had an ADHD issue. As the story goes, Hemingway had his typewriter on a mantle-like shelf so that he was standing when he was writing. Whether apocryphal or not, this is the kind of technique that Sam used to maintain the ability to stay focused and not constantly drift off and feel like he was fighting a brain fog. As you can see from Figure 2.10, Sam responded very rapidly and within 12 sessions, his Theta/Beta ratio was at a very acceptable level of 1.3.

In terms of how we treat this condition, we have a few options. In Sam's case, we reduced Theta amplitude using straightforward neurofeedback. As we will be discussing in Chapter Six, we have other more aggressive techniques referred to as brain driving. With brain driving, a child or an adult is engaged in a cognitive activity, such as reading, while we are stimulating the area of the brain associated with the specific form of ADHD or learning problem. In Sam's case, what we did was straightforward neurofeedback; he simply played a videogame with his brain. When he was able to reduce Theta amplitude, the game icons moved on the video screen.

Sam was both elated and angry at the end of treatment. This is not uncommon. Individuals are elated to find themselves in a much better position in terms of their ability to stay focused, on top of things, and sharp. However, they also are resentful and angry that something so easily resolved caused them so much grief, emotional pain, and hardship during their early childhood. This is the tragedy of our present situation in which simple procedures for assessing ADHD and other cognitive/emotional problems and the simple straightforward methods for treating these conditions have not been introduced into our schools. It should be a resource room activity. It would save huge amounts of money and reduce emotional pain and anguish for children and their families. Children would be more likely to achieve their career dreams and our jails would have more vacancies. The Swingle Clinic has many outreach programs to help with this process of introducing neurotherapy into the schools. We have had some major successes, but have also encountered huge obstacles. As one of my very wise professors told me decades ago, "Paul, it is not science, it is politics." How true and how sad. In Chapter Five, I will be discussing some efforts that are being, and have been, made to introduce neurotherapy into the school system.

THREE

Conditions That Affect Attention: Neurological

ASYMMETRIES OF THE FRONTAL CORTEX

In the last chapter, we were discussing some of the conditions that are associated with excessive amplitude in particular waveforms. In the example of the child with Common ADHD (CADD), we noted that the problem was excessive amplitude of the Theta band brain wave (frequencies in the 3–7 cycles per second range). When elevated, the child has difficulty sustaining focus because the brain is hypoactive. At marked elevations in Theta amplitude over the central part of the brain (location Cz—see Figure 1.5) we start to see evidence of hyperactivity in the child. The child is hyperactive to self-medicate. The activity stimulates the area of the brain that is hypoactive.

In this chapter, we look at imbalances between the right and the left frontal cortex. We are talking about asymmetries. Of course, excessive amplitude is also a problem, but for our present purposes we are focusing on the imbalances between the right and the left frontal cortex regions in any of the important brain wave bands.

The reason the ClinicalQ is so remarkably accurate is because it identifies imbalances and the clinical database helps us to interpret the effects of these imbalances. The very flattering remarks of Susan Olding, whose work is excerpted in Chapter One, about my ability to very precisely describe the symptoms of her child resulted largely on my interpretation of the implications of imbalances in the frontal cortex. Keep in mind that these interpretations are based on comparison of an individual's brain map with clinical databases as opposed to normative databases. As discussed earlier in this book, the important point is that the clinical database is based on the actual brain wave state of individuals who have come for treatment for very specific conditions. The predispositions indicated by imbalances in the frontal cortex have manifested, which is the reason they have come for treatment. In normative databases, un-manifested predispositions are not identified because the person is not seeking treatment. And because individuals with unmanifested predispositions are included in the normative databases, these databases are statistically blind to many of the conditions we are discussing in this book.

It is also important to keep in mind that asymmetries in the frontal cortex, although only two sites, can be very complex. If we consider only two sites and only three brain wave ranges, there are more than 100 possible permutations.

In the following section, we will be looking at some of the more common asymmetries in the frontal regions of the brain of clients diagnosed with attention deficit or attention deficit hyperactivity disorders that we see with children (and adults) who come for treatment at the Swingle Clinic. As we shall see, these asymmetries are associated with depression, anxiety, emotional volatility, oppositional behavior, and the like. These are conditions that are very frequently diagnosed as ADHD. And, as one might expect, many of these children have been medicated with very negative results, principally because they have been misdiagnosed and they have been medicated for the wrong reasons.

ASYMMETRIES ASSOCIATED WITH DEPRESSION

Asymmetries associated with dominance of the right frontal cortex (the right side of the front of the brain) are associated with depressed mood states. The right side of the frontal cortex can be more active than the left side for several reasons. For example, the right dominance associated with depression can result from conditions that make the right more active (right dominant Beta) or the left more hypoactive (left dominant Alpha). Left dominant Alpha was initially reported by Dr. Richard Davidson in a 1992 article in the journal *Brain and Cognition*, who found that individuals with elevated Alpha amplitude in the left relative to the right had a greater incidence of self-reported depression. They also responded in a more negative, withdrawing, and "depressed" manner when asked to evaluate stimuli such as music, photos, or motion pictures. When Alpha is elevated in the left relative to the right, it means that the right frontal cortex is more active than the left because the left is hypoactive. Alpha is rather like a parking frequency for the brain. When Alpha is elevated in amplitude, that area of the brain is "parked" more than the side with lower amplitude Alpha.

However, the frontal lobes of the brain can be out of balance for many reasons other than disparities in Alpha amplitude. If Theta brain waves (3–7 cycles per second) have greater amplitude in the left relative to the right frontal cortex, then the right is more active than the left. That is, because Theta brain wave activity indicates reduced activity, that part of the brain is going to sleep, so to speak. When Theta is considerably stronger on one side, it implies that that side is both hypoactive and also "not answering the phone." Its communication with other brain areas is hypoactive. Hence, this also means that the right side of the brain is more active, or more aroused, relative to the left.

Figure 3.1   Elevated Alpha amplitude in the left frontal cortex

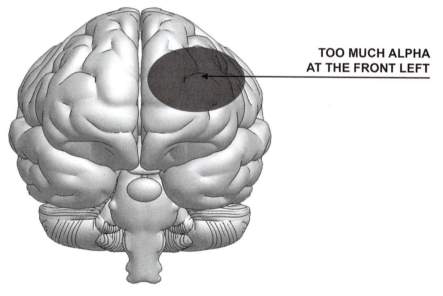

TOO MUCH ALPHA
AT THE FRONT LEFT

The brain topographs shown in Figures 3.1 and 3.2 indicate the areas of the brain where these asymmetries are found. Figure 3.1 indicates the elevated Alpha in the left side of the brain, while Figure 3.2 indicates a similar area where Theta is elevated.

Figure 3.2   Elevated Theta amplitude in the left frontal cortex

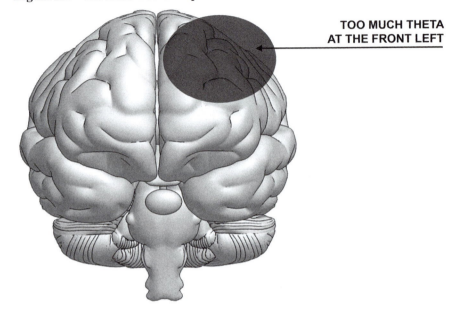

TOO MUCH THETA
AT THE FRONT LEFT

The right side of the frontal cortex can be more active than the left because the left is hypoactive, as shown in Figures 3.1 and 3.2. However, the right can be more active because it is aroused rather than because the left is underaroused. The permutation associated with elevated arousal of the right relative to the left is when Beta (brain waves between 16 and 25 cycles per second) is stronger in the right relative to the left. Figure 3.3 shows the elevated Beta in the right side of the brain that would be implicated with the elevated Beta form of depression.

A final permutation is a combination where slow frequency amplitude is somewhat higher in the left and Beta amplitude is somewhat higher in the right so that the Theta/Beta ratio (the ratio of the amplitude of the 3–7 Hz brain waves divided by the amplitude of the 16–25 Hz brain waves) also results in the right side of the frontal brain being more aroused than the left. Figure 3.4 shows the areas of Theta and Beta brain wave activity that are implicated in the Theta/Beta ratio disparity form of depression predisposition.

All of these conditions are associated with predisposition to depressed mood states. Depression is often misdiagnosed as an attention problem in children. A cardinal symptom associated with depression in young children is lack of interest, poor motivation, and inattentiveness. They simply

Figure 3.3   Elevated Beta amplitude in the right frontal cortex

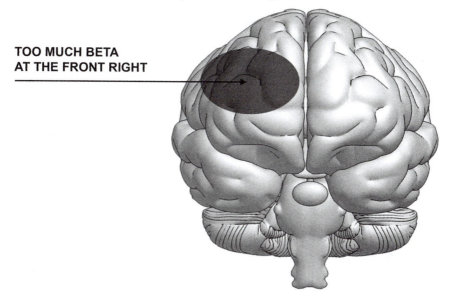

TOO MUCH BETA
AT THE FRONT RIGHT

Figure 3.4   Elevated right frontal Beta combined with elevated left frontal Theta

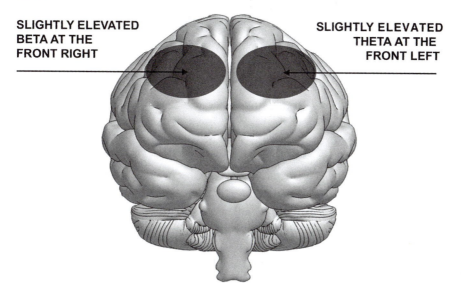

SLIGHTLY ELEVATED
BETA AT THE
FRONT RIGHT

SLIGHTLY ELEVATED
THETA AT THE
FRONT LEFT

do not have the interest or energy to be attentive, interested, or focused in school. Sometimes they also seem to be unhappy or withdrawn, but again, this can be misinterpreted as problems with focus and attention, particularly if there is a lack of motivation.

There is a difference in misdiagnosis of children versus adults. Children with a depression problem are likely to be diagnosed with some form of ADHD and given stimulants. Adults with bona fide ADHD are more likely to be misdiagnosed with depression and given antidepressant medications. So, although one of the themes of this book is, "Are you sure it's ADHD?" we must always keep in mind, "Are you sure it's NOT ADHD!" We will have a look at a case in a later chapter that dramatically emphasizes how undiagnosed ADHD in adults can have a major negative impact, not only on the person, but on the entire family.

Research is in progress to determine the qualitative differences in depressed mood states that are associated with these different asymmetries. Often we find that Alpha asymmetry is likely to be associated with what is called "reactive depression." Reactive depression is not necessarily associated with a neurological predisposition, but is a depressed mood state that is in response to some condition or event. For example, the death of a pet can be reflected in elevated Alpha in the left relative to the right frontal cortex, associated with the child's grief and sorrow. It is important to note that although one may help to console an individual going through reactive depression, it is important not to chemically sedate that process. Antidepressant medications are inappropriate for reactive depression. If someone dies, you are supposed to feel unhappy! If you do not go through the grieving process but rather sedate this normal process, you are likely to set the conditions for a lifetime of emotional problems and "need" for lifetime support from antidepressants.

Chronic medication use for reactive depression usually results in the person being trapped in the depressed state for many years after the precipitating event, simply because they have not managed the sadness and grief which is part and parcel of living through these conditions. However, we also see individuals who seem to be stuck in a reactive depression even when not medicated. These individuals often show a genetic marker for predisposition to depression which is triggered or "turned on" by a major loss, such as the death of a loved one. In such cases, treating the genetic predisposition is appropriate to help the person move forward in the grieving process. Treatments may include neurotherapy, focused emotional release therapies such as bilateral stimulation and somatic release procedures, and antidepressant and/or antianxiety medications. Skilled psychopharmacologists are invaluable in treating these disorders.

ASYMMETRIES OF ALPHA IN THE FRONTAL CORTEX

In the previous section, we reviewed the symptoms resulting from asymmetries in brain waves that are associated with right dominant arousal in the frontal cortex. This difference in arousal can be associated with elevated Alpha amplitude in the left side of the frontal part of the brain. This condition, as we noted, is associated with depressed mood states. It also is associated with correlated symptoms of lack of motivation and interest.

When Alpha is elevated in the right frontal cortex relative to the left, we are likely to see symptoms associated with oppositional and defiant behavior in the child. This condition is very likely to be misdiagnosed as hyperactivity disorder. The neurological mechanism involved is that the right frontal area in the brain is associated with theories of the self and concepts associated with social interaction and social skills. When that area of the brain is not functioning in an efficient manner relative to the left side of the brain, we find problems associated with interpersonal behavior. In young children, the tendency is for the interpersonal dysregulation to be of an oppositional and defiant nature.

It is important to keep in mind that children often go through periods of opposition and defiance. We do not want to run to the psychologist anytime a child is acting normally. However, prolonged and problematic phases may indicate that there is an Alpha imbalance so that the child is having difficulty with development of social skills, empathy, and understanding social interaction.

Attention Deficit and Attention Deficit Hyperactivity Disorders often give rise to disruptive and defiant behavior in children. But the process is different than that of the oppositional and defiant behaviors related to the Alpha imbalance referred to above. Children who are exposed to failure and constant criticism for not working and not performing up to their potential, often notwithstanding personal effort, regularly become behaviorally disruptive. And the reason is quite clear in that being seen as disruptive is far less painful than being considered stupid.

Misdiagnosis of this condition is very common. Children with ADHD, particularly the high frontal Alpha form described in the previous chapter, become severely distraught because they simply cannot keep up academically. As we have seen, with some forms of ADHD, the harder they try, the worse the situation becomes. They are angry, frustrated, belligerent, and terrified that people will discover that they are deficient. If they happen to be fortunate to have emotional security and some non-academic recognized capability such as a sport or music, then their core emotional belief about themselves may not disintegrate to self-loathing.

If they do not have the opportunity to strongly engage in an esteem-supporting activity then they frequently discover that belligerence feels good, and certainly better than self-loathing. Belligerence can, and often does, evolve into seriously aggressive and violent behavior. In addition to the potential for something like music training to help the child develop a self-esteem boosting activity, Dr. James Hudziak reports in the *Journal of the American Academy of Child & Adolescent Psychiatry* (2014) that music training actually alters brain structure related to memory, attention, and organization. He further states that because music training alters brain structure in areas associated with executive functioning it may also help kids focus attention, control emotions, and diminish their anxiety.

Hank, a 10-year-old boy, was brought to my office by both parents. Hank was pleasant, polite, and very cooperative. He smiled and joked with me and seemed genuinely interested in my describing how neurotherapy is being integrated into the training programs for many major professional sport teams.

Figure 3.5   One of the "perfect storm" profiles

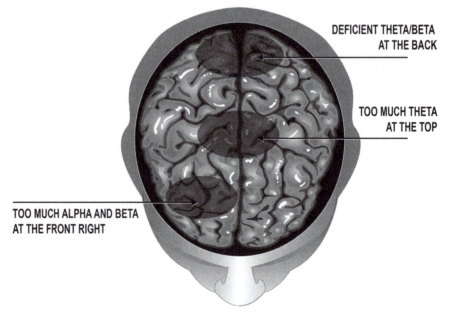

DEFICIENT THETA/BETA
AT THE BACK

TOO MUCH THETA
AT THE TOP

TOO MUCH ALPHA AND BETA
AT THE FRONT RIGHT

Hank's ClinicalQ was alarming. Recall, I do not ask clients/parents why they have sought treatment. Hank's ClinicalQ topograph is shown in Figure 3.5.

Hank has what I often call "a perfect storm." There are many "perfect storms," including those associated with depression, anxiety, and PTSD, but Hank's was perfect for an ADHD child evolving into a belligerent and eventually violent person, whose life would be a nightmare for both himself and everyone he came into contact with.

These children often present as very docile and pleasant, as did Hank. However, they also have the propensity to explode without apparent reason or warning. The afternoon after Hank's morning visit to my office, he was brought by the police to a psychiatric emergency facility. He did not want to take off his muddy shoes when coming in the house from school. He swung his school bag, hitting his mother who fell and broke her nose. Hank threw his school bag at his younger sister and was then restrained by his father until the police arrived. His father later related to me that he had been told by the social worker on Hank's case that the best way to deal with Hank's behavior was "accommodation."

Hank's perfect neurological storm included a task-related elevated Theta form of ADHD; the worst kind, in my opinion. The harder Hank tried academically, the worse things became. He also had major markers for predisposition to depression and for interpersonally antagonistic and insolent behavior. He further had the neurological marker for poor stress tolerance.

The neurological condition associated with Hank's behavior was the least of our problems. The neurotherapy would deal with these inefficiencies in brain functioning quite readily. The serious clinical challenge with Hank was his outrageous behavior, which had been very strongly reinforced. And the more outrageous the behavior, the more he gained control. I was discussing this case with an old octogenarian colleague clinician. His statement to me was: "in the old days he would be cooling his hot ass in a snow bank— then we would decide if he could achieve 20 percent cold and 20 percent hungry, or remained 80 percent cold and 80 percent hungry—to quote ancient Russian wisdom on child rearing!" He was not serious, of course, but the point was that this child needed efficient parenting with rules, regulations, and consequences with the overriding structure of positive contingent reinforcement.

Hank had been in the "system" for several years. He had been medicated with many different pharmaceutical cocktails but, short of sedation, nothing proved effective. Hank's treatment required about three years. During the last part of the second and the entire third year, he was seen in the Swingle

Clinic every month or so. The major work was done in the first year. The treatment consisted of correcting the neurological anomalies, but the major treatment was behavioral. Hank was put on a behavioral program very similar to what we do with children on the autism spectrum. A behavioral consultant visited Hank's home several times to help establish workable contingency programs. Thus, Hank's behavior had consequences so he could learn appropriate interpersonal behavior and personal emotional control.

At one point, Hank was placed in a group residence for a few weeks. He had privileges to come home on weekends if his behavior, both at the residence and at home, was acceptable; again the contingencies. The time in the residency seemed to be particularly helpful in getting Hank to comprehend and modulate his agonistic behavior.

Hank is not one of our miracles, although he is presently doing very well. He is in his final year at high school and has been accepted into a two-year community college trades program. He lives at home, has a girlfriend, is finishing high school, and has stayed out of jail! Further evidence that neurotherapy is often not a standalone treatment. Without the behavioral component, Hank would be sitting in jail even though the neurological component went very well. We do have miracle clients that appear similar to Hank in

Figure 3.6   A child diagnosed with ODD

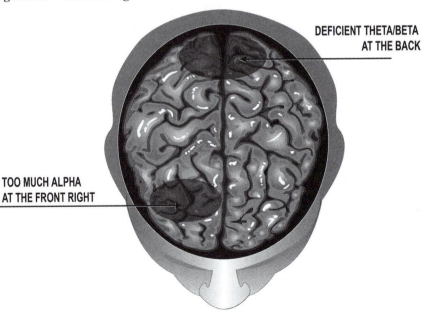

DEFICIENT THETA/BETA
AT THE BACK

TOO MUCH ALPHA
AT THE FRONT RIGHT

terms of their neurology. These clients respond remarkably well to neuro-therapy and require no major behavioral interventions.

ADHD can be the cause of oppositional and defiant behavior because of the enormous frustration and humiliation some children with this condition endure. Children can have ODD without any neurological markers for ADHD but usually they have the deficiency in the back of the brain indicating poor stress tolerance and a hyper-aroused brain. The topograph of a child with the ODD Alpha excess in the right frontal cortex is shown in Figure 3.6. Note that this child also has the deficient Theta/Beta ratio in the occipital region; a concomitant condition often found in the ClinicalQ of the child diagnosed with ODD.

ASYMMETRIES OF THETA IN THE FRONTAL CORTEX

In the previous section, we discussed the symptoms associated with conditions that result in the right side of the frontal part of the brain being considerably more active than the left. This imbalance in activity can be related to a number of neurological conditions including that of Theta amplitude being greater in the left relative to the right. Greater right side activity is related to depressed mood states, including predispositions to depression, presently occurring depression, and reactive depression such as when one suffers a loss.

When Theta amplitude is elevated in the right relative to the left, we have a condition that is associated with emotional volatility. This condition can also be similar to what we find when Alpha amplitude is elevated in the right relative to the left. The qualitative difference appears to be that when Theta is elevated, there is increased irritability or emotional volatility. Children will often cry or become upset more easily. Children and adults will be more irritable. Additionally, children with this condition will often be less capable of staying focused because of poor capability to cope with frustrating, or trying, learning tasks. This, then, can be related to the misdiagnosis of an attention problem because the child reacts emotionally to criticism, suggestions, or challenges. The presumption made by teachers and others is that the child is having an attention or focus problem and cannot stay with the task. The assumption often associated with this condition is that the child's emotionality is a reaction to the frustration associated with the ADHD. In fact, neurologically based emotional volatility is the cause not the symptom. Stimulant medication for this condition in general has very negative effects and we see many such children at the Swingle Clinic who have been prescribed off-label use of antipsychotics.

Of course, the diagnoses are quite varied for this condition as well. The elegance of the ClinicalQ diagnostic is well-demonstrated in the assessment and, usually, treatment of this condition is rapid. The prescriptive neurotherapeutic protocol for this condition is simply to balance Theta amplitude between F3 and F4.

Figures 3.7 and 3.8 show the intake topograph for Clarita, a 37-year-old woman who was told she had "histrionic disorder." I assume the diagnostician meant that Clarita had a histrionic personality disorder; a condition where histrionics serve the purpose of masking/defending against profound feelings of worthlessness.

Figure 3.7   Elevated right frontal Theta

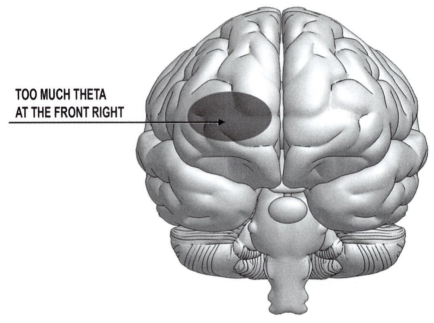

TOO MUCH THETA
AT THE FRONT RIGHT

In addition to the elevated right frontal Theta, we see that Clarita also had markers for a history of emotional trauma. We will be reviewing this situation in the next chapter, but for present purposes, the trauma marker is seen as blunted Alpha in the central/occipital regions when the eyes closed EEG is recorded for the ClinicalQ.

Clarita claimed she did not have any problems in school until she reached late high school. She also had difficulty in college but managed to graduate. She said she was given an "antianxiety" medication which she felt helped her

Figure 3.8   Blunted Alpha trauma markers

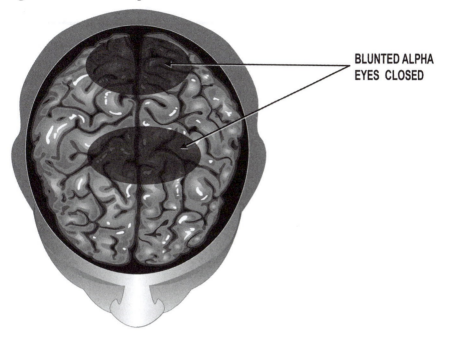

BLUNTED ALPHA
EYES CLOSED

get through university. Clarita felt that her academic problems were associated with an anxiety condition.

Clarita's condition was elevated right frontal Theta amplitude. In addition to emotional dysregulation, any imbalance in the frontal regions of the brain must, of necessity, reduce cognitive efficiency. Treatment of this aspect of Clarita's condition was straightforward suppression of the right frontal Theta amplitude. However, treatment of the sequellae of the emotional trauma required a few additional sessions of trauma release therapy. We will return to this aspect of Clarita's treatment in the next chapter.

ASYMMETRIES OF BETA IN THE FRONTAL CORTEX

The final asymmetry we will discuss in this section is that of Beta (16–25 Hz). When the amplitude of Beta is considerably greater in the left relative to the right frontal cortex, this condition is usually associated with anxiety. This appears to be a neurological predisposition to elevated anxiety as an ambient state. Poor stress tolerance is also often associated with some inefficiencies in the back of the brain, a condition we discussed earlier in this chapter. A deficient ratio of Theta to Beta amplitude in the back of the brain is also often associated with problems with attention and fidgetiness. The child cannot "shut the brain off" and the chatter interferes with focus and attention.

Imbalance in frontal Beta, however, appears to be more problematic, at least clinically, in that the person complains of severe anxiety but often without any apparent extant behavioral agitation. Elevated anxiety associated with elevated left frontal Beta amplitude is often diagnosed as an attention problem. The child cannot concentrate because of physiological discomfort associated with severe anxiety. If combined with the neurological condition of heightened emotionality, as discussed earlier in this chapter, these children, particularly when very young, are too frightened to go to school. They simply cannot tolerate the hyper-physiological arousal.

SUMMARY

Asymmetries of the Frontal Cortex

The sections on the asymmetries in Alpha, Theta, and Beta represent but a small number of the more than 100 permutations that one can observe in the frontal cortex. The skilled clinician using the ClinicalQ with the clinical database can interpret these asymmetries with great precision, and thus identify with great accuracy the child's presenting symptoms. More importantly, the ClinicalQ directs treatment, identifying the exact locations and neurology that are problematic.

In short, the diagnosis that the child walks in with should be put aside. Focus should be exclusively on what the neurology is telling us about that child. Once we get an idea of what the brain is telling us, we start our diligent search for the symptoms/conditions identified by clients which are associated with the anomalies defined. For example, if we find markers for depression, we want to find out if the child is experiencing anything that would give rise to a reactive depression, such as the death of a loved one or a pet, bullying, or some failure in attaining a desired goal.

These asymmetries can often give very valuable insights into potential family dynamic problems that may be the cause of the child's attention, behavioral, or emotional difficulties. Bullying and other circumstances that frighten or trouble the child can also often be identified. We will discuss these areas more thoroughly in the next chapter.

Multiple Asymmetries

Neurological and experiential conditions are very frequently misdiagnosed as ADHD. These misdiagnoses are what give rise to the flagrant misuse of medications because the symptoms that are being medicated are not associated with the presumptive causes. A child who is experiencing a serious fear of abandonment and lack of security because of a family problem can be severely distracted in school, suggesting an ADHD condition. One can medicate and do all kinds of treatment very ineffectively if one is not attentive to the neurological underpinnings of these conditions and, equally important, the social context and experiences of the child.

Although ADHD is a litterbin diagnosis in that children with any focus or attention issues are likely to get thrown into this diagnostic wastebasket, a related contemporary diagnostic favorite is Bipolar Disorder. I am reminded of a cartoon I saw showing two mothers with baby carriages with one mom saying "Yes, he has Bipolar Disorder." Probably true! However, it is wrong to call a developmental process a "disorder." The frontal regulatory areas of the brain are not yet "online" so the infant is highly emotionally dysregulated; the infant can laugh, giggle, scream, cry, pay attention, and ignore all within moments.

Table 3.1   Pediatric Bipolar Disorder

- Commonly starts in childhood/adolescence
- On average 3.4 medications
- On average 6.3 trials of psychotropic medications
- Highly comorbid
- Prevalence about 1/100
- Over 90% receive psychotropic medications
- Diagnosed with comorbid ADHD: Adult 3%, Child 32%

Source: Hamrin et al. (2010).

In Chapter Two, we reviewed the high frontal Alpha form of ADHD. High frontal Alpha is associated with emotional and cognitive dysregulation. When this condition manifests with significant emotional dysregulation, it establishes a neurological platform for conditions that are often diagnosed as Bipolar Disorder. We typically see some other exacerbating neurological conditions including depression markers in the front of the brain, poor stress tolerance markers in the back of the brain, and elevated activity of the anterior cingulate gryus (ACG). We also often see trauma markers with these children, as well, and early childhood trauma (e.g., a physically abusive parent) can result in an eroded core emotional belief about one's self-worth, resulting in personality problems.

As shown in Table 3.1, children diagnosed as Bipolar also have a 32 percent chance of being diagnosed with ADHD, as well. So now we enter the

"Disney World" of diagnostics. If the child catches the label ODD or Bipolar Disorder, they unhappily are likely to receive a medication for which there is scant evidence for effectiveness (see Table 3.2) and plenty of evidence for unpleasant side effects. And, as detailed in Table 3.1, they are likely to have many trials with different psychotropic medications, finally settling on a chemical cocktail containing more than three separate prescription medications.

If they are able to catch the label ADHD, then luckily, they are likely to receive a medication that has about a 40 percent success rate with somewhat less unpleasant side effects. Or if they are really lucky, in addition to catching the ADHD label, the diagnosing pediatrician is aware that brain biofeedback has been rated as a number one evidence-supported nonpharmaceutical treatment for ADHD in a report that was posted on the American Pediatric Association web-site.

Table 3.2   Unsupported Antipsychotic Use in Children

"A significant proportion of children younger than 18 years in a . . . Medicaid population (of 11,700) received a second-generation antipsychotic for conditions that have no published evidence supporting their use."

"Behavioral problems, including oppositional and conduct disorders and hyperkinetic-hyperactivity symptoms were frequently seen among children treated with . . . antipsychotics."

"Primary off-label uses for these medications are for children with behavioral problems . . . obvious and urgent need to compare the safety and effectiveness of these agents (relative to) other treatment approaches that are effective in modifying children's behaviors."

Source: Pathak, P. (2010, February). *Psychiatric Services.*

It is with these very complex conditions that the ClinicalQ assessment shows its diagnostic strength. Again, the focus is on bottom-up, not top-down. We are not interested in labels which tell us nothing and offer no information regarding treatment. We see several common patterns with children who catch the Bipolar label. Common to all is elevated frontal Alpha amplitude. The same pattern, discussed in Chapter Two, as the high frontal Alpha form of ADHD. So, rather than the question "Are you sure it's ADHD?" we should ask "Are you sure it's NOT ADHD?" Figure 2.10 in Chapter Two shows the topograph of a child with this form of ADHD. Figure 3.9 shows the topographic EEG of a child with deficiencies in the back of the brain associated with poor stress tolerance and predisposition to anxiety states.

Figure 3.9   Elevated frontal Alpha; deficient Theta/Beta at O1

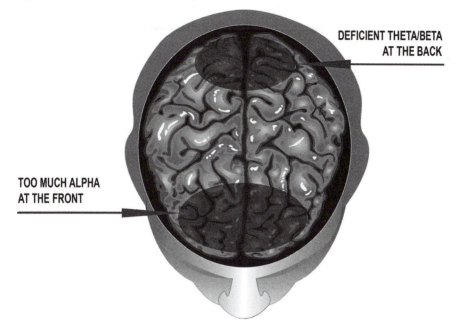

DEFICIENT THETA/BETA
AT THE BACK

TOO MUCH ALPHA
AT THE FRONT

Figure 3.10   Elevated frontal Alpha; elevated right frontal Beta

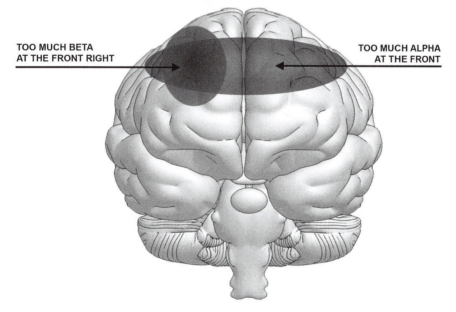

TOO MUCH BETA
AT THE FRONT RIGHT

TOO MUCH ALPHA
AT THE FRONT

Figure 3.11   Elevated frontal Alpha; elevated left frontal Beta

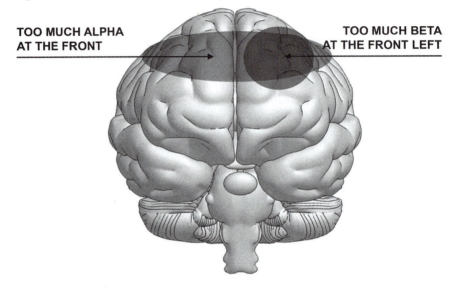

Figure 3.12   Elevated frontal Alpha; elevated high Beta Gamma frontal midline

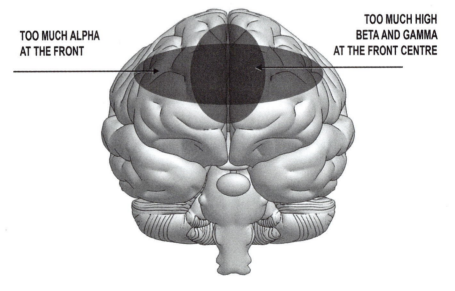

There are distinctive behavioral differences associated with the various combinations of the neurological conditions shown in the figures. Recognizing that there are several hundred distinctive profiles that are the possible combinations of just seven sites neurological characteristics (four sites and three brain wave ranges), we can say a few words about the more common patterns we observe in our clinic.

High frontal Alpha amplitude, as stated previously, is associated with emotional dysregulation. It is also associated with problems with planning, organizing, sequencing, and completing tasks. The behavior we might find is a child who has major problems in school and easily gets emotionally distraught when her dysregulation evokes teacher/parent critical attention. The emotional dysregulation associated with the high frontal Alpha is apparent in each of the other combinations of the neurological anomalies, as shown in the figures.

High frontal Alpha combined with deficient Theta/Beta ratio in the occipital region of the brain as shown in Figure 3.9 is an emotional child who shows major signs of anxiety, cannot sit still, and often has sleep problems. The child shown in Figure 3.10 is likely to be unhappy, have poor motivation, and be emotionally volatile. The child shown in Figure 3.11 is likely to be the most highly anxious showing many anxiety symptoms, whereas the child shown in Figure 3.12 is likely to also show symptoms of behavioral perseveration similar to OCD patterns.

PROBLEMS WITH SLEEP

The data are very clear. Sleep problems with children have very serious consequences. Many clinicians accept the notion that "if you fix sleep you fix everything." Overdrawn, of course, but nonetheless, sleep disruption in children markedly affects their school performance, as well as many other aspects of their lives.

This review of sleep problems could have been included in the following chapter that focuses on experiential factors effecting children's cognitive and emotional well-being. Factors such as poor sleep hygiene, family strife, and addiction to electronic media are all experiential and can have very severe detrimental effects on sleep. Many of these factors will be discussed in the next chapter, but sleep is directly related to neurological factors as well. More often than not, it is a combination of neurological and experiential factors that must be considered. Often we find that the problem of too little sleep is related to experiential factors such as texting with friends late into the night. Poor sleep architecture, in contrast, is likely to result from neurological factors, recognizing of course that if the child does not go to bed, sleep architecture will be affected.

In a study of over 14,000 children followed over a period of almost five years, published in *Pediatrics* (September 2012), Dr. Karen Bonuck and her colleagues report that children with behavioral sleep problems are seven percent more likely to have special educational needs. This number gets even higher if the problem is sleep-disordered breathing, where the percentage of children needing educational assistance jumps to 38 percent.

A review article by Chiu, Nutter, Palmes, Pataki, Johnson, Tegene, and Windle on pediatric sleep disorders (published online on *Medscape*, March 2012) states: "Learning difficulties, emotional lability, attention deficits, disruptive behaviors, social and school impairments, family dysfunction, low self-esteem, depression, anxiety, cognitive dysfunction, hyperactivity, irritability, and memory impairment represent common comorbidities of sleep disorders in children and often exert bidirectional or reciprocal influences. [Sleep apnea may also] lead to pulmonary hypertension, right-side heart failure, growth retardation, and failure to thrive." Similar findings with adults, with and without ADHD, reported by Arns, Feddema, and Kenemansm in *Frontiers in Human Neuroscience* (December 23, 2014) indicate a direct and continuous relationship between self-reported sleep problems and inattention.

So, sleep problems are neither trivial nor benign (see Table 3.4). We also know that some of these difficulties are not neurological but reflect differences in cultural changes regarding our view of the importance of sleep for the developing brain. Children today obtain about one hour less sleep per night than they did just 30 years ago. The effect of this is lowered IQ and poorer performance, among other health issues. Bronson and Merryman report, in their book *NurtureShock: New Thinking About Children*, that research shows that "the performance gap caused by an hour's difference in sleep was bigger than the gap between a normal fourth-grader and a normal sixth-grader." In high school, there is a steep decline in sleep hours, and a striking correlation of sleep and grades.

In just a few decades, our sleep patterns have changed markedly. In teenage years, adolescents are getting an hour less sleep than they used to; an hour less than what they really require to function adequately. In addition, the introduction of blue-light electronic devices such as cell phones, ipads, and eReaders can markedly interrupt sleep particularly when used immediately prior to bedtime. Dr. Chang and her associates report in the *Proceedings of the National Academy of Sciences* (December 2014) that ipad use immediately before bedtime reduced melatonin levels and increased levels of self-reported tiredness and inattentiveness the following morning.

Table 3.3   Required Sleep Time

General guidelines

1–4 First Month

15–16 hours per day
Newborns typically sleep in short periods of two to four hours. Premature babies
may sleep longer and colicky ones shorter.

1–4 Months Old

14–15 hours per day
During this period more regular sleep patterns often start to develop. Sleep
periods start to run four to six hours and often more regularly in the evening.

4–12 Months Old

14–15 hours per day
Establishing healthy sleep habits is a primary goal during this period, as the child
is now more social with more adult-like sleep patterns. Establishing regular
naps, one in the morning and one in the afternoon, generally happens at the latter
part of this time frame, as biological rhythms mature.

1–3 Years Old

12–14 hours per day
Most children from about 21 to 36 months of age still need one nap a day, which
may range from 1 to 3½ hours long. They typically go to bed between 7 and
9 p.m. and wake up between 6 and 8 a.m.

3–6 Years Old

10–12 hours per day
Bedtime continues typically to be between 7 and 9 p.m. and wake up around 6 to
8 a.m. At 3, most children are still napping, while at 5, most are not.

7–12 Years Old

10–11 hours per day
At these ages bedtimes gradually become later, with most 12-year-olds going to
bed at about 9 p.m.

12–18 Years Old

8–9 hours per day
Sleep remains vital to health and well-being for teenagers as when they were
younger. Many teenagers may need more sleep than in previous years.

Table 3.4   Sleep Architecture

Restorative sleep is not just a matter of hours in bed. The amount of time in each of the stages of sleep is critical to restorative sleep. Although each stage of sleep in the sleep cycle is important, deep sleep (stages 3 and 4) and REM sleep are particularly important.

Deep Sleep

The most damaging effects of sleep deprivation are from inadequate deep sleep. Deep sleep is a time when the body repairs itself and builds up energy. It plays a major role in maintaining health, stimulating growth and development, repairing muscles and tissues, and boosting the immune system. To wake energized and refreshed, sufficient quality deep sleep is critical.

REM Sleep

Deep sleep renews the body; REM sleep renews the mind. REM sleep plays a key role in learning and memory. During REM sleep, the brain consolidates and processes the information learned during the day, forms neural connections that strengthen memory, and replenishes the supply of neurotransmitters, including feel-good chemicals, such as serotonin and dopamine that boost mood during the day. REM is also believed to be central for dealing with the day's emotional events. In the Swingle Clinic, we find that many clients who have problems with unprocessed emotional trauma have deficient REM sleep. When the traumas are resolved, REM sleep tends to increase.

Disrupted sleep interferes with our ability to process information properly and our mood states are affected, revitalizing bodily functions are affected, integration of what we have learned for adequate recall is affected, and our ability to process and integrate the emotional experiences of the day is affected. It is difficult to stress just how important adequate sleep is, particularly for the young developing brain.

As we will discuss in the next chapter, sleep hygiene is as critical as neurology for children to get adequate sleep. Internet addiction is a major problem often causing severe sleep deprivation. We will go into more detail later about this sleep disruptor.

Oversleeping can be a serious problem as well, but one that we are less concerned about with children. With older people, oversleeping can seriously affect mood states and, in particular, cognitive efficiency. The interesting feature of oversleep is that the more one sleeps, the more tired one becomes. Excessive sleep is a depressant and sleep deprivation can have antidepressant effects. However, excessive sleep is less of a problem for children. The exception to this is when oversleep is associated with depression. Depression with young children often manifests as lack of motivation, tiredness, and lack of interest in activities. This condition is usually identified on the ClinicalQ brain wave assessment.

If your child is not getting the amount of sleep indicated in Table 3.3, before you do anything about any presumed attention deficit difficulty, restore proper sleep hygiene. Set a fixed bedtime, pay attention to nutrition and eating times, and reduce television and video game exposure. If your child's attention difficulties are still apparent after you are convinced that sleep hygiene is adequate, then seeking some professional assistance may be appropriate. Remember: sedated sleep is not sleep. The treatment for poor or inadequate sleep is not to medicate but to correct sleep hygiene.

If sleep quality remains a problem, then neurotherapy is the recommended treatment. Often a sleep assessment is obtained along with the ClinicalQ EEG assessment. The sleep assessment is obtained with a wireless EEG unit that clients take home and use for about four nights. This provides a more reliable sleep assessment than the four-hour snapshot sleep assessments generally obtained in the sleep assessment labs. We see what the sleep architecture looks like over four nights, for the entire sleep cycle, and in the familiar home environment. We can also see the effects of medications, as well as sleep-enhancing products that we use in the Swingle Clinic. One such sleep aid is a sound that the client plays throughout the night. Compared with the sedating sleep medications that reduce sleep onset for insomnia patients by about 22 minutes, the harmonic sleep aid reduces sleep onset by about 17 minutes. So with the sleep monitors, we can test sleep aids to determine their efficacy.

Some common poor quality sleep architecture profiles are shown in the sleep assessment records presented in Figures 3.13–3.16. The areas in the top quadrant are periods of being awake, the next quadrant is light sleep, the third quadrant is REM sleep, and the bottom quadrant is deep sleep.

Neurotherapy is very effective for treatment of sleep disorders; again, stressing that sleep hygiene is critical as well. Most clients with sleep disturbance have deficient Theta/Beta ratio at the back of the brain and correcting this can markedly improve sleep. Other sleep problems are associated with depression markers in the brain, although it is more likely that the depression is the symptom of poor sleep, and not the other way around. Dysregulation in the Alpha brain waves, likewise, can be associated with poor sleep quality. The common high frontal Alpha form of ADHD, for example, is often associated with REM sleep problems, whereas excessive Beta in the

Figure 3.13   Sleep record of client with good sleep architecture for REM and Deep Sleep

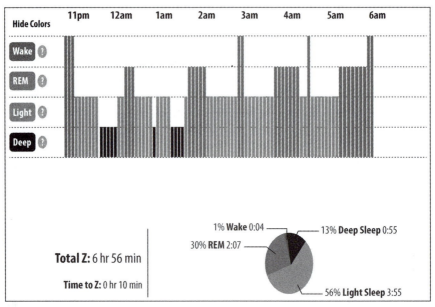

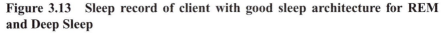

Figure 3.14   Sleep record of client with oversleeping profile

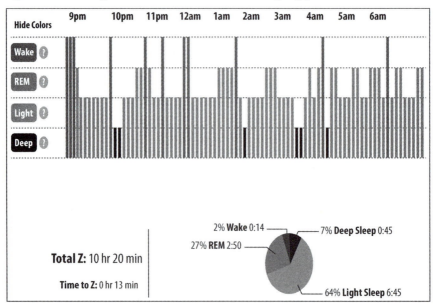

Figure 3.15   Sleep record of client with deficient REM and adequate Deep Sleep

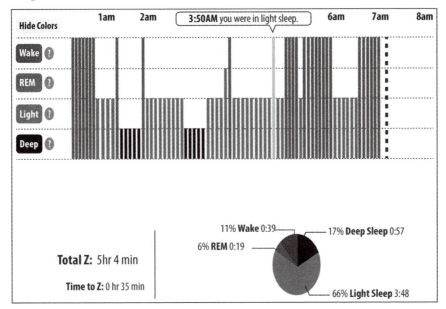

Figure 3.16   Sleep record of client with good sleep architecture for REM but deficient Deep Sleep and excessive waking

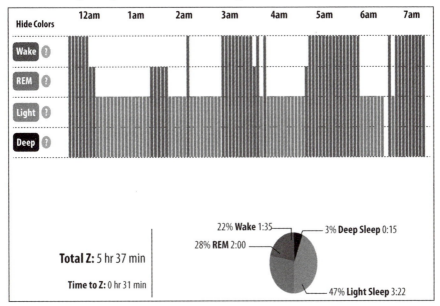

back of the brain, under eyes closed conditions, is often associated with deficient deep sleep.

Although the focus of this review has been on neurology, it is important to reiterate that many sleep problems are caused by experiential factors. Sleep duration has decreased for children over recent decades to the point where it is estimated that about one third of children in the United States suffer from inadequate sleep. Research from Finland (*Sleep disturbances and psychiatric symptoms in school-aged children*, Academic Thesis, University of Helsinki, 2004) by Dr. Juulia Paavonen indicated that children whose average sleep duration was less than 7.7 hours had many of the same symptoms as children with ADHD. In particular, this research indicated that short sleep duration is associated with behavioral problems because of the effects on hyperactivity and impulsivity.

"GO TO BED!" Clearly an experiential factor; parents have a responsibility to set the rules and make sure the child complies. Irregular bedtimes disrupt natural physiological rhythms and can undermine normal maturation in the developing brain. Research published in the medical journal *Pediatrics* (October 2013) by Dr. Yvonne Kelly and her colleagues on data from over 10,000 children found clear associations between irregular bedtimes and behavior. Irregular bedtime was related to hyperactivity, conduct problems, emotional problems, and problems with peer relationships. These effects worsened over time. But, if bedtimes were regularized, these conditions improved. Obviously, the sooner the bedtime is regular, the less enduring the cognitive and emotional problems.

MILD TRAUMATIC BRAIN INJURY (TBI)

All kids hit their head. When is it serious? Of course, if the child shows symptoms of disorientation, loss of consciousness, vomiting, loss of verbal fluency, and the like, the child is rushed off to the family physician, or the emergency room. But what about the many day-to-day knocks? It is very difficult to assess the cumulative effects of repeated head impacts.

Table 3.5 provides a list of symptoms resulting from mild traumatic brain injury (TBI). How can something be "mild" and "traumatic?" By *traumatic* we mean neurologically measureable and by *mild* we mean that the symptoms are mild. For example, we would consider the symptoms mild if the child has problems with attention, even if it is serious lack of attention, but the child does not suffer from a condition such as ataxia where there is compromise of motor control. As evident from the table, there are a number of symptoms of TBI that mimic ADHD. These include problems with attention and concentration, the symptoms of the elevated slow frequency amplitude form of ADHD, described earlier. The symptom of difficulty with planning is shared with the elevated frontal Alpha amplitude form of ADHD, also discussed earlier.

Table 3.5   Symptoms of Mild Traumatic Brain Injury

Headache	Irritability
Chronic Pain	Mood Swings
Dizziness-Vertigo	Personality Changes
Difficulty Concentrating	Hemiparesis
Difficulty with Attention	Palsies
Difficulty Planning	Aphasia
Effort Fatigue	Visuospacial Impairments
Anxiety	Changes in Appetite
Depression	Sensitivity to Hot and Cold
Sleep Disturbances	Seizures

At the Swingle Clinic, we see many children who have been diagnosed with ADD, ADHD, ODD, LD, ASD, and many other acronyms. The common behavioral difficulties shared by many of these children include problems with attention, problems with learning, problems with getting along with others, oppositional and defiant behavior, and problems with impulse control. Based on the specific combination of these "problematic" behaviors as judged by parents and teachers, the healthcare provider—physician, psychologist, school counselor, and the like—attaches one or more of these acronymic labels and recommends "treatment." The treatment usually includes a medication, a special school program, and often counseling to help the family cope with the problematic child. The problem with such a procedure is that the health provider likely neglected to consider a very important acronym, TBI.

As we have discussed, the common characteristic symptoms associated with TBI include problems with concentration and attention, difficulty with planning and organizing, problems with anxiety and depression, sleep disturbances, mood swings, and problems with impulse control, irritability, personality changes, and visual/spatial impairments. Misdiagnosis of children with TBI is very common. For example, in an article published in the *Journal of Adolescent Health* (2014), Drs. Chrisman and Richardson reported that adolescents with a history of concussion had a three-fold increased risk of being diagnosed with depression. Since a diagnosis is usually based on the child's behavior, healthcare providers routinely diagnose these brain-injured children as having ADHD, ODD, developmental delay, depression, autism or Asperger's, or one of the many learning disorders. Many of the symptoms are identical to those of the other diagnostic categories. The huge advantage of neurotherapy in the treatment of children is that the brain mapping procedure provides a precise indication of the exact location of the problem in the brain and the exact nature of that problem. Hence, true ADHD has one of several specific brain wave patterns, which are quite distinguishable from TBI.

Children (as well as adults) with TBI virtually always have some difficulties with symptoms associated with damage to the frontal regions of the brain. Because of the way the brain sits in the cranial vault, any head injury, no matter where the impact, affects the frontal cortex. Injury to the frontal cortex is routinely associated with problems with emotional volatility, impulse control, learning difficulties, personality and mood problems, and problems with attention, planning, organizing and following through on tasks. Does the latter sound like ADHD or ODD? You bet, but drugs like stimulants, antidepressants, or antipsychotics simply exacerbate the problems of these brain-injured children.

It is also important to note that the symptoms associated with TBI can persist for months if not years. Dr. Slobounov and colleagues report in *Clinical Neurophysiology* (2012) that residual brain dysfunction as measured by both EEG and physical balance are measureable one year post mild injury. This is important to keep in mind because a child may show symptoms of ADHD long after a mild knock to the head and this episode is forgotten by parents or not considered as cause of the attention problems.

The following is the case of Mike, a nine-year-old child who was referred with the diagnosis of ADHD and/or ODD. His problem was, however, TBI. Most children are frightened when they walk into a doctor's office and Mike was no exception as he grumpily entered my office with his weary looking father. Despite his heroic efforts to conceal his unease, Mike's eyes widened as he saw all of the electrodes and other electrical gadgetry in my office.

Kids are not the only ones who become concerned when they see the electrodes that I intend to attach to their heads. The first thought is usually: "He's going to give me electroshock therapy." So my first task when starting therapy with any of my clients is to assure them that the electrodes are for the purpose of measurement only. They are attached to the head with a paste, the consistency of toothpaste, in order to measure the electrical activity of the brain. The client feels absolutely nothing but can see the electrical activity coming from the brain displayed on the computer monitor.

Always directly addressing the child whenever possible, I asked Mike, "Do you know what I do?" "Sort of. You do something to my brain," he replied. "Well," I said, "Mike, sort of. I set things up so you can do something with your own brain. You might think of me as a coach. Coaches, or neurotherapists, as we call ourselves, help you make your brain more efficient, kind of like a trainer helps football players strengthen their bodies. By the way, part of what I do is work with professional athletes." I could see his eyes light up in interest. "A lot of super athletes do neurotherapy because it makes them much better at their game. I expect that you may do some optimal performance training at some point if you continue training with me here in the clinic."

"What we'll do today is have a look at how your brain is functioning. I will do that by attaching a wire to each of your ears, and one on top of your head that I will move around from place to place." Doubt entered his eyes, and I reassured him, "You won't feel anything. We are simply measuring the electrical activity of your brain. You'll be able to see your brain activity on the computer monitor. I'll ask you to open and close your eyes at various times, read something for a minute or so, and I'll also play a sound that sounds like 'shush.' It takes about fifteen minutes, and then I'll do some calculations and go over it with you in detail to see if what the brain is telling me is the same as what you experience."

I was watching Mike's father out of the corner of my eye. Parents are usually focused on telling their tales of woe regarding the incorrigibility of their child, their long suffering tolerance and their willingness to make "one final attempt to help—provided the child will make a serious effort, etc. etc." The serious behavioral consequences of brain injury can be extremely disruptive to positive family functioning. Resentment, anger, defiance, and disappointment are all direct consequences of the family dynamics that are associated with the child's disruptive behavior. The child is usually told that he is not working hard enough, when in fact he is doing the best he can. This inevitably leads the child to conclude that he is stupid, worthless, and unlikable. The problems with impulse control, explosive anger and rages, and severe mood swings further confuse and alienate the child. Defiance and other forms of acting out can also be vain efforts to protect themselves from their core emotional belief about themselves. And self-loathing is not too strong a term to describe the emotional pain of these children. In this regard it is interesting to note the work of Dr. Keith Yeates and his colleagues reported in *Child Neuropsychology* (2010) indicating that positive and supportive family environments can moderate the psychosocial outcomes of TBI.

One element of neurotherapy that parents, and older people in general, feel unsettled about is the notion of changing the way the brain functions. Changing brain functioning is completely at odds with what we have been taught; namely, that what you were born with is what you must live with. We were also taught that after a brain injury, recovery was limited to about 18 months. After that time, there would be very limited improvement. We now know that the brain is very plastic and brain inefficiencies can be corrected long after the TBI. Dr. Jonathan Walker, a Board Certified Neurologist, reported in the *Journal of Neurotherapy* (2002) the results of some of his work with TBI clients whom he treated between 3 and 70 months post TBI. Dr. Walker reported that 88 percent had a 50 percent or greater improvement in symptoms. So, it is clear that significant improvement can be achieved with neurotherapy more than five years post injury. Dr. Walker's data indicate also that symptoms associated with TBI persist for years post injury.

Although I was talking directly to Mike, his father was trying to enter the conversation to inform me about Mike's problems. Instead, I told Mike, "The brain is going to tell me everything I need to know about why you are here. After we go over the results of the brain measurements, if there is something I've missed, you can let me know, OK?" I said to Dad, "If there is anything Mike or I miss, please let us know."

I have Mike's attention. He is sitting forward in his chair and looking directly at me. His sullen behavior, at least toward me, is gone, and he is eyeing the items in my office. I explain to Mike that to measure his brain activity, we are going to attach a wire to each ear with a plastic clip and attach one to his head with a little paste. He will feel nothing because we are only measuring the brain activity; similar to the way a doctor listens to his heart. I asked Mike to sit in a chair facing the computer monitor, and then I cleaned his earlobes with an alcohol wipe with a bit of abrasive to remove oils and dead skin. For children Mike's age, I usually just say that they will feel the cold of the alcohol and a scratching sensation when I clean the scalp. For younger children who still seem frightened, I usually say "ouch" when I first touch the earlobe with the alcohol wipe. Inevitably, they laugh and say it did not hurt.

"OK, Mike, we are about ready to start. As I said, the measurements will take 10 or 15 minutes. You will feel nothing, and you can watch the electrical activity coming from your brain on the monitor in front of you. I will ask you to open and close your eyes at various times. I will also ask you to read something (for nonreaders I usually ask them to count if they can), and I am going to have you listen to a sound. When we are finished, I will remove all of the paste from your head and ears and then do some calcula-tions on your measurements. We will then go over what the brain is telling us about your strong areas and areas where you might have some difficul-ties. It is very important that you remain as still as possible during the measurements. Every few minutes I will stop the measurements so you can move around if you wish." For young children I refer to these pauses as "wiggle breaks."

The measurement phase is very short, consisting of 2½ minutes of record-ing on top of the head, 1 minute at the back, 45 seconds over each of the two frontal lobes in the brain, and finishing with 60 seconds of recording over the middle of the front part of the brain. This adds up to six minutes of actual data recording, but moving electrodes, printing the data, and chat-ting with the child usually takes approximately 15 minutes in total. Most neurotherapists try to make use of every moment of contact with the child. While moving the electrodes, one might chat about sports they play, favorite pastimes, and things they collect. I have many objects in my office, includ-ing old bottles, arrowheads, sharks' teeth, and old money. The child usu-ally becomes intrigued by these things, and I then introduce "Dr. Swingle's Treasure Chest," which contains all sorts of wonderful things, including dinosaur bones, coins, stamps, paper money, semiprecious stones, and fos-sils but no toys, candy, or other silly trinkets. The child is told that at the end of every session they can take one of the items from the treasure chest. This not only serves as a reward but also supports the educational model of the treatment. After their treatment, the child is intellectually sharp. The items in the treasure chest are all labeled and have a short informative description of the item. Also, on the wall above the chest are world maps, geological calendars, and sample charts, so the child can identify, date, and locate any item in the chest. And because of their mental state, they do not forget the material. Often they bring these items in to school for show-and-tell, frequently startling teachers about the breadth of their knowledge about these items.

While the measurements are in progress, I also speak softly to the child, placing my hand on their shoulder and reinforcing them for cooperative participation. I am also instructing the parent, to some extent, in that they observe me directing the child in a firm, but kind, manner. I speak to them with obvious interest but do not permit disruptive behavior. Occasionally, we run into parenting situations that are outrageously out of control, such as a parent who has obviously abrogated her or his responsibilities about who makes the decisions. Such situations definitely require family therapy in addition to neurotherapy. Fortunately, in Mike's situation, his father, although angry and worn out, understood the need for parental authority and responsibility.

Likewise, the reading material that I use to measure a cognitive challenge is thematically important. The brief excerpts include stories of the first human on earth, when all the animal tribes spoke one language; brothers who loved each other so much that they secretly shared their food with each other without the other's knowledge; and that being good at something does not mean being perfect but rather failing less often.

"Now, that was painless, wasn't it?" I said to Mike as I removed the electrodes and cleaned off the electrode paste from his head and earlobes. "Did you think I was going to zap you with the electrodes?" Mike was smiling now and highly interactive. He said that when he first saw the "electric stuff" he thought I was going to "electrocute him." I then asked Mike to sit next to me at my desk while I reviewed his brain map numbers.

Neurotherapists generally provide a great deal of detail during an initial evaluation. This part concerns mostly the parents, but the child is kept as strongly engaged as possible during the review. I explain that some brain waves are associated with slower activity in the brain, such as daydreaming; other brain waves are associated with brain efficiency; others with trauma; and still others with processing information. Children hear so much bad news when they go to physicians and psychologists, school counselors, and teachers. They are told that they are not behaving properly; not performing at their level of capability; are lazy, disruptive, and not nice to be around. They are told that they need help, if only they would try, and maybe they should be in a special-needs program. The message is—you're stupid and unlikeable!

I always start off with the positive features found in the brain map, and there are always good things to be found. In Mike's case, I was very lucky to see that his brain showed the "artist's signature." "Hey, Mike, look at this. Do you like to draw, or build things, or write or play music? This is the artist's signature in the brain." I could tell by the look on the father's face and by Mike's smile that I was "batting a thousand." "He's always drawing and building stuff," said Dad enthusiastically. "He used to be crazy about Legos and now he builds models—he also takes apart a lot of things and forgets to put them back together." He looked at me curiously. "How did you know that about Mike?" I responded, "The brain tells us everything," a concept I repeat over and over during the first session. I showed Mike and Dad the artist's signature, which is a very large increase in a particular brain wave when the client closes their eyes. "Mike," I said, "that is an extremely valuable skill to have. Good artists, architects, choreographers, and fiction writers have that signature, and so do fine cabinetmakers and good mechanics. You're a lucky kid. You will probably pick a career that uses that skill." After reviewing the areas of brain functioning that are within normal limits, I zero in on the reason the child has been brought to my office. The reason Mike was brought to my office was because he was highly disruptive in school and at home and had been given the diagnosis of ADHD. His father also revealed that a psychiatrist had also suggested that Mike might also have ODD.

Mike had a very mild case of a form of an attention problem that I have found more often in males than in females. In Mike's case, the indicator was a slight excess of slow-frequency brain wave amplitude over the top of his brain. This excessive amplitude became a bit worse when he read. As I showed this to Mike and his father, I asked Mike, "In class, do you have problems staying with the teacher?" Mike nodded. "Do you find yourself thinking about other things when the teacher is talking?" He kept on nodding. However, the brain also revealed something else that was far more serious than a very mild ADD condition. Mike showed major slowing of brain wave activity in the frontal regions of the brain. There are several measures of frontal cortex injury, such as increased amplitude of slow frequency brain waves including Delta (1–3 Hz) and Theta (3–7 Hz). Slowing of the Alpha band (8–12 Hz) and imbalances in frontal areas are also found. The emotional and behavioral consequences of these brain inefficiencies can be major. They include violent outbursts, rage, marked defiance, depression, severe impulse control problems, severe cognitive and memory deficits, major mood and personality changes, and poor moral compass.

These behaviors have nothing to do with ADHD or ODD or LD or any of the other diagnostic labels stacked on top of these children. I explained to Mike's dad that these conditions could be corrected with neurotherapy. The same electrodes used in the assessment would be placed on Mike during treatment sessions. The electrodes were again for measurement only, and Mike would not feel anything. We would set up the treatment so that when Mike's slow brain wave amplitude declined, Pacman would move on the screen. By concentrating, Mike would slowly learn to reduce the amplitude to the normal range. This procedure is straightforward neurofeedback (brain wave biofeedback), a form of conditioning in which the brain learns by being reinforced for specific responses. When the brain makes a desired response, Pacman moves. The same procedure would be used to increase the dominant Alpha brain wave frequency and to balance the activity in the frontal brain regions. Both of the latter conditions (i.e., slowing of the dominant Alpha brain wave frequency and imbalances in the frontal regions) are common conditions found with clients who have frontal brain injury.

I also prescribed a recorded sound CD that Mike could use at home while doing homework. It would suppress the slow frequency brain wave amplitude as well as speed up the dominant frequency in the Alpha band. Suppression of the slow frequency amplitude would help him concentrate and retain information and the increasing of the dominant Alpha frequency would increase brain efficiency. The CD contained the harmonic sound that I had tested during Mike's assessment. The sound had instantly suppressed the slow frequency by 22.1 percent, so I knew it would work before I prescribed the CD. In addition, the specific harmonic also has the effect of increasing the dominant frequency of the Alpha band as well as suppressing the excessive Theta amplitude, which is of major benefit to clients with TBI. In an article published in the *Journal of Neurotherapy* (Swingle, 1996), I reported that the specific harmonic that was prescribed for Mike suppressed Theta amplitude by over 30 percent, on average, for a clinical sample of clients with TBI.

Mike needed 26 sessions to normalize the slow brain activity. He soon was reporting that with the exception of one C, his grades were "great." The balancing of the frontal lobes and the increasing of the dominant Alpha brain wave frequency required an additional 22 sessions. Mike's negative thought patterns, his oppositional behavior and, in particular, his impulse control problems and inappropriate social behavior were markedly improved, based on reports not only from Mike, but also from his parents and teachers. His relationship with his father was much better.

Disorders like TBI are not just problems for the individual; they should be considered family disorders. Many problems, other than those directly resulting from TBI, including alcoholism, depression, anxiety, chronic pain, attention deficit disorders, and age-related declines in memory affect the entire family as well as friends. Further, fixing the neurology of a problem may not resolve the psychological issues associated with the disorder that can have debilitating effects on people. Neurotherapy is not a stand-alone treatment. Clients and their families need complementary therapies to deal with the psychological baggage associated with all disorders. This is particularly true of clients with TBI. TBI clients are often seriously disordered in terms of mood modulation, anger/aggression/rage behavior, and serious deficiencies in terms of impulse control.

Just imagine if Mike had been 40 years old before he came for treatment. He might well be alcoholic or addicted to some other substance or harmful behavior, at a career dead end, unsuccessful at multiple relationships, angry, depressed, and believing that he was a defective human being. Individuals with TBI have earlier age of onset of drug abuse, longer duration of substance-use disorder, and are more likely to progress from alcohol abuse to another drug-use disorder. Criminal behavior seems to be more likely for persons with TBI. In one study, Dr. Lewis and colleagues reported (*American Journal of Psychiatry*, 1988) that 100 percent of a sample of inmates on death row had evidence of TBI, and numerous studies have found that incarcerated males are very likely to have frontal lobe injury.

There is another side of this issue that is also important. Consider the older Mike, now in a troubled marriage, who is in marital counseling with his wife. The counseling does not seem to be going anywhere, and Mike and his wife are likely to end up being one of the statistics of over 50 percent failure rate in marital counseling. Why? The marital counselor is missing a big part of the problem. There is a family disorder of TBI that manifests itself in alcohol abuse, anger problems, and career failure. The marital counselor is likely to be considerably more successful if the whole problem is treated. The brain inefficiencies are corrected with neurotherapy, and the interpersonal problems are dealt with in marital counseling. Mike might also benefit from some individual therapy focused on important life changes, including treatment for self-destructive addictive behavior and career counseling.

As Mike's case indicates, many common disorders, including learning problems, ADHD, depression, anxiety disorders, sleep problems, as well as serious problems such as TBI, can be effectively, safely, and permanently improved or corrected with procedures that help the brain regain normal functioning. Neurotherapy is a drug-free, self-regulation treatment that corrects problems in the brain. Medications do not correct problems like those associated with brain injury but rather just mask or sedate the problem, often with serious side effects.

Although Mike's behavior would suggest a diagnosis of ADHD or perhaps ODD, it was apparent to me that the major cause of Mike's difficulties was TBI. The brain map did not show the common patterns associated with these diagnoses other than a very minor ADHD pattern. Mike's brain did show a slowing of the Alpha frequencies and slow frequency amplitude excess in the frontal regions. There are other patterns associated with TBI as well, including excessive high frequency amplitude and problems with brain site to brain site communication, referred to as coherence. Whenever we suspect TBI because of inconsistency between brain patterns and reported behavior, such as ADHD, we always do a full 19 point brain map and compare the data from that map with our databases. The database comparisons show how the brain data in question differs from normally functioning brains. This analysis can be remarkably detailed, showing the interconnecting activity between all 19 sites as well as detailed analysis of one cycle per second bands of activity.

The remarkable aspect of neurotherapy is that these departures from normal brain functioning can be markedly improved by focusing on the exact brain activity shown to be abnormal in the maps. What is even more remarkable is that we have proven that what we were taught in medical and graduate schools just a few years ago, and is still believed by a discouragingly large proportion of the medical and psychological health provider community, is simply wrong. Brain injury is treatable. Further, the notion that after about 18 months post trauma there will be minimal further recovery is just wrong! Compelling evidence, such as that of Dr. Walker discussed earlier in this chapter, shows that with proper neurotherapeutic treatment, further recovery can be realized years after the brain injury. Recent research on brain plasticity at some of the world's most prestigious universities shows conclusively that recovery of brain function can occur at any time if proper treatment procedures are employed AND you do not further damage the brain with sedating drugs.

Further discussions with Mike's family revealed that Mike had experienced a serious head injury from a fall when he was about five years old. The conventional wisdom, at the time, was that he probably sustained a concussion and his young brain would recover—no big deal! It was further revealed that Mike had a number of other "whacks on the head" which were all assumed to be quite normal for a healthy and active male child. TBI can be cumulative. A child can have several head impacts that appear to have no residual effects and then a minor head impact that results in behavioral changes. Because the critical last head injury appears to everyone to be trivial, it is logically assumed that the problem is not related to brain damage. Obviously, the severity of the head injury is an important issue, but the age of the child when the injury occurred is also extremely important. We always seemed to assume that the younger the brain, the greater the recovery potential.

Researchers at the University of Melbourne, Australia, report that there is a direct relationship between severity of the injury and recovery of cognitive functioning. However, what these researchers also report is that the amount of recovery from severe TBI was considerably better for older children (Rosema et al., 2014). Recovery for infants to about two years of age was minimal after severe injury whereas better outcomes were observed for older children with injuries of comparable severity. Further, younger children with moderate TBI likewise did poorer than older children with comparable injuries. These findings indicate that we need to modify our thinking about head injuries in infancy. The research on brain plasticity indicates, on the one hand, that the brain has remarkable capability for recovery and improvement in function after TBI, even many years post incident. On the other hand, the evidence indicates that very young children may be particularly vulnerable to TBI, resulting in significant intellectual impairment.

Although the evidence is limited at this time, it would seem advisable for parents to have a neurotherapeutic assessment and treatment for infants who have sustained head trauma. In the Swingle Clinic, we see many very young children who respond well to a nonvolitional form of neurotherapy, developed in this clinic, which I call *braindriving*. This procedure involves direct-loop stimulation of the brain with light and/or sound that is completely dependent on brain activity. For example, if the amplitude of slow frequency in a specific area of the brain increases above a set threshold, then lights at specific frequencies and/or sounds are presented to suppress that activity. This procedure is based on behavioral conditioning techniques and has the effect of normalizing brain functioning for clients who have limited ability for volitional procedures. Such clients would include infants, children with autism or severe fetal alcohol syndrome, those who are developmentally delayed, or those who have a severe TBI.

Children who have sustained a mild to moderate TBI as an infant may show up at the Swingle Clinic at age 11 with a diagnosis of ADHD or ODD or ASD. The parent assumes that the infant had the normal bumps and knocks and so does not see the TBI as implicated in the child's cognitive and behavioral problems. Although neurotherapy can be remarkably effective in the treatment of TBI, it is important to be aware that the treatment of brain damage may require considerably more sessions and that recovery may not be as complete as in the case of, say, ADHD that is not a result of TBI.

Parents are often not accurate at detecting brain injury because they assume that the problems they see with their child are the result of some other cause such as ADHD, bad influence from peers, or poor discipline from parents. As the reader will recall from the list of symptoms of TBI, many of these symptoms are the same as for conditions such as ADHD, ODD, autism or Asperger's, and the like. The best red flag for a possible brain injury is a sudden change in behavior, including mood changes, emotional volatility, impulse control problems, aggression, and cognitive functioning. If you see rapid onset of one or more of these symptoms, TBI should be considered.

Finally, if the red flag appears, remember that conventional MRI, CT Scan, and visual EEGs as commonly used in hospital environments are very likely NOT to reveal any noticeable damage. Dr. Provenzale pointed out in an article in the *American Journal of Roentgenology* (2010) that neither CT scan nor MRI was efficient at detecting TBI, or predicting cognitive deficits and at 1-year follow-up were not found to have predictive value for clinical outcome. The quantitative EEGs used by neurotherapists, and now many hospitals, are very effective for revealing areas of functional difficulties in the brain.

Uncorrected brain irregularities are likely to deteriorate into the problems we discussed in the case of the mature Mike, regardless of the original source of the brain inefficiencies. However, behavioral problems resulting from ADHD do seem to be more controllable with behavior therapy, whereas similar problems resulting from TBI do seem to be far less modifiable with behavioral control methods. The injury has to be treated with neurotherapy for the child to be able to efficiently respond to the behavioral control programs put in place by parents and teachers.

Misdiagnosis associated with TBI is most serious in young children. There are several reasons for this. The first is that we assume that all children have bumps and knocks and that, by and large, they recover perfectly adequately without any serious long-term negative effects of their injuries. And these are the children who come in with diagnoses of ADHD when, in fact, it is a condition associated with the brain injury.

In my experience, the problem of misdiagnosis is less serious with adults. Adults are aware of the fact that they have had a head injury and they are also aware of cognitive effects of these injuries. They tend to be more aware of feeling more sluggish, less sharp, less "on the ball," and so forth. The more serious issues that we confront with TBI with adults are the serious disorders of mood and emotional regulation. Our prisons are loaded with individuals, primarily males, who have frontal lobe injuries that result in violent and aggressive outbursts, poor impulse control, and severe mood swings. However, we do get a number of individuals who do not identify their cognitive decline with a head injury. This is particularly true with older clients who have been led to believe that what they are experiencing is normal age-related decline, when in fact it is either caused by, or exacerbated by, a TBI. One of the effects of TBI is a slowing in cognitive efficiency, a condition that mimics age-related decline.

Dr. Gerald Gluck (personal communication) shared data showing the decline in the Alpha peak frequency over the course of a three-year period of a former football player who sustained serious concussions. This football player had not received any neurotherapeutic treatment for the concussion. Over the three-year period there was a progressive decline in the peak frequency of Alpha. At first measurement, the Alpha peak frequency was in the range of 11 cycles per second, which is an efficient, fast Alpha peak frequency. The peak frequency declined to 9.5 cycles per second after about two years and to 8.5 cycles per second after three years, which is a very slow peak frequency. And as we have discussed, slow Alpha peak frequencies correlate with poor cognitive efficiency.

Referring back to the list of characteristics associated with TBI shown in Table 3.5 it is easy to see how children, in particular, can be misdiagnosed. Although our main focus is ADHD, it is also easy to see how children with TBI can also be misdiagnosed as having ODD, explosive aggressive problems of various sorts, developmental delays, and even autism because of the effects of the injury on the frontal part of the brain. It is important to keep in mind that because of the way the brain sits in the cranial vault, almost any impact to the head no matter what direction the impact is from, generally has some effect on the frontal cortex. Thus, in addition to attention issues, children with TBI are very likely to show effects on mood volatility, emotional regulation, and impulse control that are very frequently misdiagnosed. It is also easy to see that many of our dropouts from school were children who spent a good part of their childhood school life in detention or in the principal's office, and may well have had untreated TBI.

The problem tends to be less severe in adults in the sense that adults are likely to be more mindful of the relationship between an injury and dysregulated mood states. However, often individuals with head injury are not aware of the direct relationship other than what people around them are able to observe and tell them. Again, to repeat, our prisons are overloaded with individuals whose crimes may well have been the direct result of undiagnosed and untreated TBI. It was very encouraging to learn that ClinicalQ assessment has been admitted as evidence in a capital murder case in the state of Florida. Dr. Gluck, source of the TBI data described earlier, was instrumental in having the QEEG admitted in evidence in this death penalty case (reported in *Biofeedback*, 2011).

FETAL ALCOHOL SPECTRUM DISORDERS

Children with milder forms of Fetal Alcohol Disorder (FAD) are often misdiagnosed with ADHD. Unlike children with the more severe conditions who have facial deformities such as wide set eyes and smooth upper lip, those with the milder form do not have the facial deformities but exhibit cognitive, behavioral, and motor deficits. The children we see at the Swingle Clinic with FAD are typically brought in by grandparents and adoptive or foster parents. Grandparents often are aware of or suspect an FAD problem but adoptive parents are frequently unaware of the prenatal conditions of the child.

Biological mothers of mild FAD children will often admit to what they believe were safe drinking levels during their pregnancy. Popular belief is often that having a glass or two of wine every once in a while has no serious consequences. The evidence is overwhelming that this is simply not the case. Alcohol exposure from the mother's drinking affects brain development and disruption of neural networks that negatively affects not only thought and cognition but also can negatively affect vision, hearing, touch, balance, motor skills, language, and emotion.

Because of the disruption of the neural networks, prenatal exposure to alcohol can also result in behavioral disorders. Thus, in addition to misdiagnosis of ADHD, we often see children with mild FAD diagnosed with conditions such as oppositional and defiance disorders and other conduct disorder diagnoses.

Figure 3.17 shows the compromised areas in brain function of an 11-year-old child with mild FAD. There are many profiles that we see with mild FAD that are associated with different levels of exposure, prenatal phase of exposure, and other contributing factors such as diet, genetic predispositions, and emotional care. As we see in the figure, this child shows marked elevation of slow frequency amplitude in the front part of the brain and elevated Theta in the back area of the brain. In addition to the areas shown in the figure, there is Alpha slowing all over the cortex which is a common condition found with the FAD child.

Although the limited ClinicalQ can identify FAD, we always do a full 19-point brain assessment with these conditions. The reason that a full Q is required is because FAD involves problems with neural connectivity which can only be identified with simultaneous recording of all 19 brain locations. In addition to the negative effects on learning, attention, and focus, prenatal alcohol exposure also can give rise to elevated levels of anxiety and disengaged behavior, a condition we often find in children with the high frontal Alpha form of ADHD.

So, what is a safe level of alcohol consumption during pregnancy? This is nicely summarized by Dr. Kelly Huffman, senior author of the recent scientific report on prenatal ethanol exposure that was published in the *Journal of Neuroscience* (2013). In the on-line *ScienceDaily* (December 3, 2013) she stated: "Would you put whiskey in your baby's bottle? Drinking

Figure 3.17   Child with mild FAD

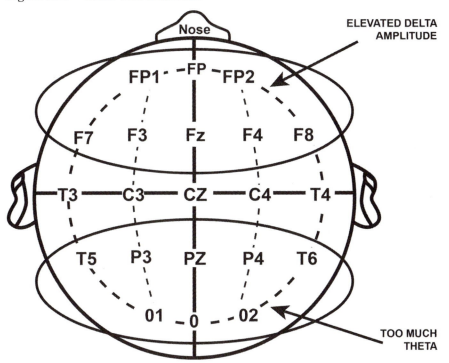

during pregnancy is not that much different," she said. "If you ask me if you have three glasses of wine during pregnancy will your child have FASD [Fetal Alcohol Spectrum Disorders], I would say probably not. If you ask if there will be changes in the brain, I would say, probably. There is no safe level of drinking during pregnancy."

SEIZURE DISORDERS

Although the treatment of epilepsy is beyond the scope of the present book, we should comment on one form of seizure found in children coming to the clinic with the diagnosis of ADHD (inattentive). Children with mild forms of absence seizure conditions often appear to be inattentive. However, because the absence seizure is mild, the child's seizure behavior does not appear sufficiently aberrant to prompt teachers and parents to investigate conditions other than the wastebasket ADHD diagnosis.

Mild absence seizures have the appearance of deep distraction. The child appears to be profoundly absorbed in thought or daydreaming and may require multiple prompts to regain awareness of present surroundings. But, because the seizure is mild, the child regains awareness relatively rapidly. However, on closer scrutiny, one finds that the child appears to be looking through you. The eyes are not focused and delayed fixation on your face seems prolonged beyond what one would expect with simple daydreaming.

Figure 3.18   EEG topograph of child with absence seizures

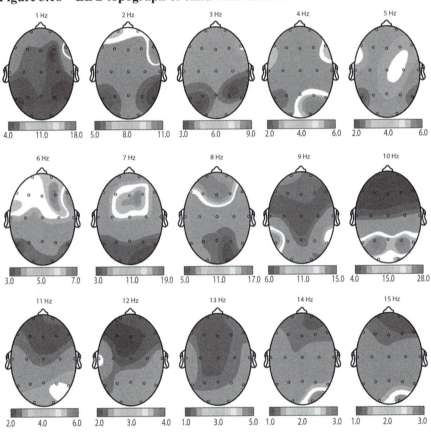

Whenever we suspect a seizure disorder, a full 19-point QEEG is required. There are many features of the full EEG that are relevant to the treatment of seizure disorders, including epileptiform spiking and problems with the interconnectivity of brain areas. We screen for possible seizure and related conditions with the shorter general purpose intake ClinicalQ. The statistic of interest is the ratio of the strength of slow frequency amplitude brain waves to a specific brain wave found over the Sensory Motor Cortex (location Cz).

The specific brain wave is called the Sensory Motor Rhythm (SMR) and it is in the range of 13–15 Hz. This elevated ratio can be seen visually in the EEG topograph shown in Figure 3.18, where slow frequencies in the 6–8 Hz range are elevated (light areas) and the 10–15 Hz are low (darker shades).

AUTISM SPECTRUM DISORDERS

There is a very high correlation between autism disorders and seizure disorders. Estimates vary a bit but a reasonable estimate is that about 25 percent of children on the Autism Spectrum (ASD) have a seizure disorder as well. We see many children with Lennox–Gastaut Syndrome (LGS), a form of childhood-onset epilepsy that most often appears between the second and sixth year of life. This form of epilepsy is characterized by different seizure types and often attention problems, cognitive delays, and behavioral problems.

The more pronounced states of ASD and seizure disorders are readily identified and unlikely to be misdiagnosed and treated as ADHD. However, milder forms of both of these conditions are often misdiagnosed and medicated. Generally, medications appropriate for bona fide ADHD are either not effective or, more often, exacerbate the cognitive/behavioral difficulties of these children.

Three features of brain functioning often found in the cases of mild ASD, and in particular, mild forms of Asperger's are elevated slow frequency amplitude in the back of the brain (location O1), imbalances in Alpha amplitude between F3 and F4, and elevated fast frequency amplitude in the frontal midline (location Fz) of the brain. The summary of the ClinicalQ of just such as child, let us call him Siegfried, is shown in Figure 3.19a.

Siegfried was a remarkably bright child. However, his teacher was concerned because Siegfried was often in "his own world" and he found it difficult to get him to focus on the classroom activity. Siegfried was also very rigid and became very upset if schedules were changed. At home, he had to have things very much in order. His clothes for the next day had to be laid out with his shirt on top of the pile and his socks on the bottom. There were other examples of the obsessive-like behavior. Siegfried was also very much a loner. He stayed by himself during playtimes and was awkward and uncommunicative when put in group situations, such as for group projects in the classroom.

The elevated slow frequency amplitude in the back of the brain is associated with problems with staying in the present. This is shown in Figure 3.19a where the eyes open Theta/Beta ratio at the back of the brain is 2.94. Ratios above about 2.2 are usually indicative of some problem with staying in the present. Deeper than a daydreaming state, more like fugue, children, like Siegfried, repeatedly drift off and lose concentration. They are difficult to refocus and have difficulty remaining refocused.

Siegfried's asocial behavior is associated with the elevated Alpha amplitude in the right frontal area of the brain. This is the area of the brain associated with the "theory of self" related to the ability to be empathic and social skill acquisition. In Figure 3.19a, the imbalance between the right (F4) and the left (F3) fontal regions is 22.5 percent. The areas of the brain associated with these conditions are shown in Figure 3.19b.

The elevated higher frequency brain wave activity over the frontal midline is associated with over-activity of the ACG, shown in Figure 3.20,

Figure 3.19a   Summary of ClinicalQ assessment for child with mild Asperger's

Cz: Theta/Beta = 2.19; Theta/SMR = 3.90
O1: Theta/Beta (Eyes Open) = 2.94
Fz: Delta = 13.0; HiBetaGamma/Beta = .74; Sum = 17.8; L/H Alpha = 1.10
F3 & F4: Theta/Beta F3 = 2.09, F4 = 1.93; F4 > F3 Alpha = 22.5%

Figure 3.19b   Topograph of brain wave amplitudes for a child with mild Asperger's

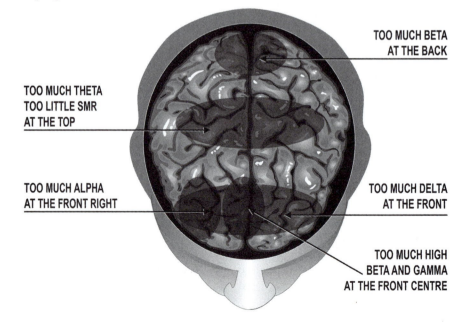

Figure 3.20   Sagittal section of the brain

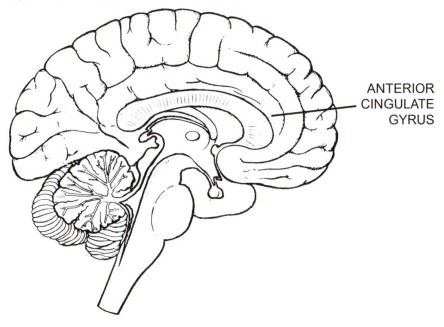

ANTERIOR
CINGULATE
GYRUS

where the 28–40 Hz/Beta ratio is 0.74. Values above about 0.55 are generally associated with cognitive perseveration. The ACG is the same area of the brain associated with obsessive and compulsive behaviors. It is the forward part of the ACG that is associated with the rigidity of thought and behavior found in the Asperger's child.

Mild ASD children can be treated very effectively with neurotherapy. Medicating this condition is not very effective, in general, and can cause some additional problems for the child, such as slowing down cognitive efficiency. Often diagnosed as ADHD because of the apparent inattentiveness, the neurological inefficiencies are more complex than ADHD. Neurotherapeutic treatment is very effective because it is data driven so that the relevant brain areas can be precisely identified and treated.

The interested reader will find the book by Arlene Martell, shown in Figures 3.21a and 3.21b, to be inspiring. In her book, Martell describes the enormous challenges parents face when trying to get appropriate treatment for children with severe cases of ASD and related seizure disorders. When Martell's son Adam was an infant she was told there was little hope. An inspiring story of a very courageous mother—the picture on the cover is Adam in his graduation tuxedo!

Figure 3.21a   "Getting Adam Back" by Arlene Martell. (Used by permission of Arlene Martell)

Website: www.EpilepsyMoms.com

Figure 3.21b   "Getting Adam Back" by Arlene Martell

Chapter 8: Neurotherapy

- Education in the Classroom – F.V. Epilepsy Society
- Magnetic Therapy
- Meeting Dr. Swingle
- What is Neurotherapy?
- Neurotherapy – A New Beginning
- Benefits and Resources for Neurotherapy
- Psychologists' Report
- Final Visit to Children's Hospital
- Life's Lessons – Holding On When Things Get Tough

www.epilepsymoms.com

VISUAL FUNCTION DISORDERS

Children diagnosed with ADHD show a significantly greater number of visual symptoms as compared with non-ADHD children as reported by Dr. Ryan Farrar in the journal, *Optometry*, in 2001. These visual problems include problems with binocular and accommodative responses, visual memory, and spatial orientation. As Dr. Hanni Hagen and colleagues point out in the *Journal of Behavioral Optometry* (2008), inefficient visual skills can interfere with attention and consequently interfere with executive brain function, reflecting the same symptoms as ADHD.

Children coming to the clinic with a diagnosis of ADHD who do not show any of the neurological patterns associated with this condition may be referred to a behavioral optometrist for assessment and treatment. We also may treat this condition with visual tracking exercises that we are able to do at the Swingle Clinic. However, in keeping with the purposes in this book, it is important to keep in mind that many children who come in with a diagnosis of ADHD actually have some other condition that is responsible for their poor scholastic performance. Again, this speaks to the power of the ClinicalQ assessment because it identifies children who do not have any of the neurological characteristics associated with any of the forms of ADHD. When we see this lack of ADHD brain wave patterns, we go through a checklist of alternative causes of the child's academic difficulties. And this certainly includes problems with sensory processing such as problems with the visual processing system.

CONCLUSIONS

When we are treating children for ADHD symptoms, we always alert parents to the potential negative impact of poor diet, possible food allergies, and inadequate physical exercise. These are particularly important for hyperactive behaviors. If children do not respond rapidly to the neurotherapy, then we are doubly suspicious of problems caused by diet, foods, inactivity, and poor quality or amount of sleep. In the next chapter we will be examining many non-neurological conditions that affect a child's ability to be attentive that are not ADHD.

Although the focus here is on the brain functioning, it would be remiss not to mention that identifying, mollifying, and correcting the difficulties children endure rely heavily on concerned, caring, and gifted teachers and clinicians, and most importantly, on unselfish, loving, and dedicated parents.

FOUR

Conditions That Affect Attention: Experiential

In general, it is appropriate to assume that any child having a problem with being attentive in school has an associated experiential problem, in addition to neurological factors. As I have pointed out throughout this book, many of the problems a child is having with regard to performance in school has little to do with the neurological condition. Also, the child's experiences in school and at home may be the experiential conditions that activate a neurological predisposition.

Children get bored, they need activity, and they go through all of the emotional ups and downs that we adults go through. We are so prone to medicating the child that we often overlook many of the experiential factors that may be primarily responsible for the child's difficulties. Again, as I have said previously, it is perfectly clear that we are medicating normal children's behavior and, in my judgment, this is an outrage.

In this chapter, we will be reviewing a number of the situations that can give rise to a child's problems in school. The list is long and we will simply be covering some of the more prominent factors that we find affect the child's ability to perform efficiently in a school context.

OPPOSITIONAL DEFIANCE DISORDER AND PSEUDO-ODD

Children with the more severe form of ADHD associated with marked elevation of slow frequency (Theta) amplitude are very likely to be hyperkinetic.

They simply cannot sit still and, subsequently, are likely to get into difficulty in school for hyperactivity and classroom disturbances. Male children, in particular, are vulnerable to developing behavioral problems associated with this more severe form of ADHD; a condition I like to call "Pseudo-ODD."

Treatment of this condition usually takes longer, for several reasons. First, it tends to be more severe neurologically in that the elevated slow frequency amplitude is greater. However, equally important is that the hyperactive child is very likely to have developed behavioral patterns that are problematic. Male children, in particular, are likely to have been routinely disciplined for disruptive behavior. They also are very likely to have been reinforced for this behavior. They receive lots of attention from everyone—teachers, administrators, parents, and in particular their classmates—for being oppositional and defiant. The secondary gain can result in the problematic behaviors developing a "life of their own" in terms of the child being rewarded for disruptive behavior. Thus, fixing the neurology may not be sufficient to fix the problem. Additionally, efficient parenting is crucial and behavioral treatment is often necessary to adequately correct the problem.

Hence, the ODD diagnosis and rush to the medicine bottle for an off-label use of an antipsychotic or antiepileptic to control behavior. Of course this is misguided and outrageous for all sorts of reasons. First, medicating behavior is just wrong. We have become intolerant of children's behavior so we medicate (sedate) behaviors we find troublesome. There are well-established methods for dealing with problematic behavior of children. It is called "parenting." And responsible teachers likewise have learned behavioral methods for dealing with children's behavior.

For the bona fide emotional/behavioral pathologies, medication combined with skilled behavioral/psychological interventions can be a very effective treatment regimen. Bona fide pathologies are very rare. The rapidly exploding rate of prescribing off-label use of antipsychotics for children speaks for itself. We have abrogated our responsibility, to our children, to be accountable for unselfish parenting and teaching. Reaching for the bottle of antipsychotic to numb the shrill of a child has all the same logic as reaching for the bottle of alcohol to numb the shrill of life.

The evidence supporting the safe use of these medications is sketchy at best. Further, there is scant evidence for the efficacy of these medications for the treatment of behavioral problems. In a *Psychiatric Services* (2010) article, pharmacist Prathamesh Pathak reports the results from records of a Medicaid population of 11,700 children under the age of 18. He comments that a significant number of children received a second-generation antipsychotic for conditions that have no supporting evidence for their use.

Further, behavioral problems, including oppositional and defiant disorders and hyperkinetic-hyperactivity symptoms, were frequently seen among the children treated with second generation antipsychotics. The central issue here is that we are medicating behavior rather than focusing on behavior modification. Results from the research of Dr. Julie Zito and colleagues, shown in Table 4.1, further emphasizes the extent of this epidemic of treating behavior with drugs. It is also interesting to note, from this study, that the use of such methods, with children from the poorest families and non-White families, is disproportionate.

This trend for off-label use of medications to treat behavioral conditions is not limited to antipsychotics. As reported by Dr. Allen Tran and his colleagues in *Psychiatric Services* (2012), the use of anticonvulsants to treat "disruptive" behavior disorders rose sharply in a national sample of youths up to 17 years of age over a 14-year period survey. The use of anticonvulsants for seizure disorders over this 14-year period remained stable but the use for behavioral disorders rose 1.7 fold.

Table 4.1   Antipsychotic Use Skyrockets in America's Poorest Children

1. "Awareness of the expanding use of antipsychotic medications in the emotional and behavioral treatment of children has been noted in several studies of community-based pediatric populations."
2. Analyzed data for 456,315 youths aged 2 to 17 from Medicaid-eligible families
3. From 1997 to 2006, use of antipsychotic medications in this population increased 7- to 12-fold, with most of the increased use associated with treatment for behavioral problems.
4. Highest increase was for children from poorest families.
5. The proportion of children using antipsychotics increased significantly more among African Americans and Hispanics than among Whites.

Source: Dr. Zito et al. (2013, March).

The increased use of antipsychotic medication to treat behavioral problems in children means an increase in the diagnosis of ODD, or other diagnostic labels, for problematic behavior. The choice of treatment method is driving the increase in the incidence of these "disorders." The distinction between bona fide ODD and pseudo-ODD is based on neurology. However, even this is moot! Children get into trouble and mischief for all kinds of reasons. Their behavior is influenced by the neurology but similar behavior patterns can evolve for different neurological reasons, depending on the experiential factors.

On the one hand, a child who has a form of ADHD and becomes frustrated, irritable, and disruptive can develop ODD-like behaviors because of the reinforcements the child receives coincident with the behavior. On the other hand, a child can develop ODD-like behaviors because of an imbalance in the amplitude of slow frequency in the frontal regions of the brain, as described in Chapter Three. This imbalance is associated with emotional volatility and interpersonal defiance. Both patterns of behavior are very much alike but need very different neurological treatments, as guided by the ClinicalQ assessment. Behavioral contingencies to modify this behavior, however, may be identical.

BULLYING

While we tend to focus our attention on the victim of bullying, we should keep in mind that the bully is generally not making out well in school. There are all sorts of reasons why children get into bullying and we will be looking at some of these factors in the following pages. Bullying is an extraordinarily serious problem in schools. Bullying can take many forms. The form that we usually think about, of course, is the male bully who threatens children in the playground by being aggressive and threatening harm. This form of bullying is usually the easiest to deal with. The bullying is obvious and apparent to teachers and there are some very straight-forward things that school teachers and administrators can do to minimize the negative impact of these bullies. Often, however, this form of aggressive physical bullying takes place outside the context of, and the purview of, teachers and school administrators. The bullies very often will be threatening their victims with severe consequences if they tell their parents or teachers about the situation.

More insidious forms of bullying, and far more difficult to control, are those that we traditionally identify with females. However, it is very prominent with male children as well and appears to be on the increase (see Mari Swingle's book *i-Minds* [2015] for data on this and related issues). These types of bullying take the form of social isolation and social humiliation. Children are victimized based on their physical appearance, physical challenges, ethnicity, culture, social status, and so on. These children are isolated and made to feel they are deficient, unlikable, and unimportant. This form of bullying is very difficult to identify and control. Children cannot be ordered to accept other children within their social groups. So dealing with the child who has been socially isolated and humiliated can be extraordinarily challenging to parents and school authorities.

In my day, the bully was the big lug in the school yard who tried to make life miserable for his school mates or the clique of children who humiliated and harassed a child with an identifiable difference. The world has changed and now we have the cyber bullies. Because of the social structure of the cyber world, parent's ability to monitor and control this medium is difficult. Data are scarce regarding the details but we do know that the impact of this form of bullying can be very severe. In recent years, for example, there have been media reports of several suicides as a result of this form of bullying.

A study in the American Medical Association journal *Pediatrics* (2014) by Dr. Frank Elgar and associates reports on the effects of cyber bullying in a sample of almost 19,000 students, ages 12 to 18, in a Midwestern state in the United States. About one-fifth (18.6%) of the sample had experienced cyber bullying in the previous year. The more frequent the bullying the greater was the chance of a reported mental health or substance use problem. The most common mental health problem reported was depression (18.9%). Reported suicide attempts were 4.8 percent and prescription drug misuse was 6.4 percent. Teens who were most bullied, compared to those who had not been bullied, had twice the likelihood of having been drunk, vandalized property, and had suicidal thoughts; three times the odds of binge drinking, high anxiety, and suicide attempts; and more than four times the likelihood of misusing prescription and over-the-counter drugs.

In the Swingle Clinic we see many children who are referred with a diagnosis of ADHD whose difficulties in school turn out to be primarily the result of being the victim of bullying. It is in these contexts that the ClinicalQ brain assessment is extraordinarily valuable. First of all, the brain assessment may identify that there are no neurological conditions serious enough to be the cause of the child's difficulties in school. Second, the brain wave activity is often very sensitive to conditions that reflect exposure to serious emotional stressors. The ClinicalQ is also sensitive to reactive depression and problems of an interpersonal nature.

Figures 4.1 and 4.2 show the brain wave assessment of a child who is suspected to be a victim of bullying. In Figure 4.1, the circled area, showing the blunting of Alpha (18.78%; should be above 30%) at a location directly in the center of the head, is a marker often associated with individuals who have been exposed to severe emotional stressors. Whenever we see this in a very young child, the two things that come to mind are bullying and family conflict. The second remarkable feature in this child's EEG, is a mild elevation of the Theta/Beta ratio over the center part of the brain. This ratio is 2.47 and anything above 2.2 or so is associated with attention problems. In this case, we have a child in which we have a minor marker for an attention problem but, more importantly, we have a marker that indicates that this child has been exposed to emotional stress.

Figure 4.1   EEG of the central and occipital brain areas of a bullied child

CZ	VALUES	% Change
EO Alpha	8.61	
EC Alpha	10.23	
% Change EO to EC Alpha > 30%		18.78%
EO Alpha Recovery	9.27	
% Change EO - Alpha Recovery		7.63%
Theta Amplitude EO	15.76	
Beta Amplitude EO	6.50	
EO Theta/Beta	2.47	
Theta Amplitude Under Task (UT)	13.69	
Beta Amplitude UT	5.89	
UT Theta/Beta	2.32	
% Change T/B EO to T/B EO UT		−6.45%
% UT Beta Increase		−10.29%
Total Amplitude	30.65	
Theta Amplitude preceding Omni	14.42	
Theta Amplitude with Omni	13.15	
% Change in Theta with Omni		−9.68%
Alpha Peak Frequency EC	10.00	
Alpha Peak Frequency EO	9.80	
Theta/SMR EC	3.15	

O1	VALUES	% Change
Alpha EO	6.16	
Alpha EC	12.06	
% Change in Alpha EO to EC		95.84%
EO Alpha Recovery	5.70	
% Change EO - Alpha Recovery		−8.16%
Theta Amplitude EO	10.09	
Beta Amplitude EO	5.17	
Theta/Beta EO	1.95	
Theta Amplitude EC	10.46	
Beta Amplitude EC	6.99	
Theta/Beta EC	1.50	
% Change T/B EO to T/B EC		−30.21%
Alpha Peak Frequency EC	10.00	
Alpha Peak Frequency EO	9.90	

Moving on to Figure 4.2, we see that there is a very large disparity in the Alpha amplitude in the frontal cortex with Alpha being considerably stronger in the left relative to the right. As discussed in Chapter Three, this is a marker for depressed mood states. We also noted in the previous chapter that when the disparity is in the Alpha brain wave range, we usually think of this as experiential in nature (that is, reactive) as opposed to neurological.

Another brain wave feature that we see in the ClinicalQ is a major imbalance in the amplitude of Theta in the front of the brain, where the right is considerably greater than the left. Again, as noted in Chapter Three, this is a marker for emotional volatility. So, based on the ClinicalQ assessment, I am developing hypotheses: this child may be exposed to bullying; he may have difficulty in school because of the mild attention issue; and he is emotionally depressed because of his poor performance academically and

Figure 4.2   EEG of the frontal brain areas of a bullied child

F3 & F4 (ALL EC)	VALUES		% Difference
	F3	F4	F3-F4
Theta Amplitude EC	10.10	16.93	
Beta Amplitude EC	6.37	7.06	
EC Theta/Beta	1.59	2.41	
% Diff F3 T/B - F4 TB EC			50.93%
Theta Amplitude EC	10.10	16.93	
Alpha Amplitude EC	13.47	9.28	
EC Theta/Alpha	0.75	1.83	
EC Total Amplitude	29.95	33.26	
*F4><F3 Beta	6.37	7.06	10.74%
*F4><F3 Alpha	13.47	9.28	−45.2%
*F4><F3 Theta	10.10	16.93	67.56%

FZ (ALL EC)	VALUES
Delta (2Hz)	10.05
HiBeta Amplitude	3.89
Beta Amplitude	6.15
HiBeta/Beta	0.63
Sum HiBeta + Beta	10.04
LoAlpha Amplitude	5.20
HiAlpha Amplitude	3.61
LoAlpha/HiAlpha	1.44
Alpha Peak Frequency	9.40

exposure to bullying. Further, the emotionality markers suggest that this may be a child who is highly emotionally reactive and may cry very easily. Of course, with his hypersensitivity, he would be a prime target for a bully.

So, to summarize the results of the ClinicalQ brain wave assessment thus far: this child has a mild marker for an attention issue; he has a marker for exposure to severe emotional stressors; and he is showing a marker for reactive depression that may be associated with some event, or circumstance, to which the child has been exposed. Figure 4.3 shows the areas of the brain that are implicated, and similar to the data contained in the ClinicalQ shown in Figures 4.1 and 4.2, there is too much Theta in the right frontal areas, too much Alpha in the left frontal areas, mildly elevated Theta/Beta ratio over the sensory motor strip, and too little Alpha response over the central midpoint of the brain.

The child with this neurological profile is a prime candidate not only for bullying but also for severe health care mismanagement. If this child is medicated for the attention issue with a central nervous system stimulant, it could easily exacerbate this child's emotionality. This may give rise to further medication to try to modulate the heightened emotionality. We see many children in this kind of situation in which there has been an effort to medicate symptoms of inattentiveness. The inattentiveness of this child is not a neurological condition related to ADHD or a mood disorder. Rather, the symptoms are associated with the child's experience of being threatened and humiliated in school. This child cannot pay attention because he is afraid. His mild attention problem is exacerbated by the fact that he cannot attend because of fear. Secondarily, the reaction to the bullying has given rise to imbalances in the front part (reactive depression) of the brain

Figure 4.3   Topograph of implicated brain regions of a bullied child

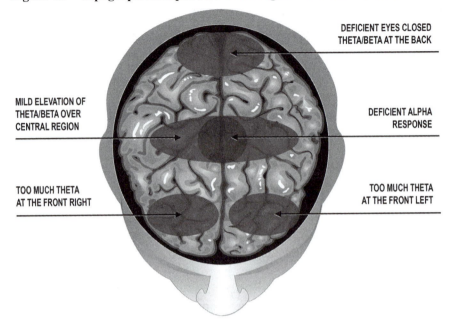

DEFICIENT EYES CLOSED
THETA/BETA AT THE BACK

MILD ELEVATION OF
THETA/BETA OVER
CENTRAL REGION

DEFICIENT ALPHA
RESPONSE

TOO MUCH THETA
AT THE FRONT RIGHT

TOO MUCH THETA
AT THE FRONT LEFT

which in turn affects cognitive efficiency, further exacerbating his academic performance, and so on, and so on. In short, this is an example of the problems we can create if we use a top-down rather than bottom-up method for assessing the child's problems. We are very likely to get into a situation in which the attention problem is medicated and the child is given some remedial educational work and perhaps concessions for test-taking. But we completely miss the fundamental problem, which is the child's emotional security.

It is clear that the major work that has to be done for this child is to get the bullying under control. From a neurological perspective, there are a few things that we can also do to help. First, we would reduce the Theta/Beta ratio over the central part of the brain to reduce the mild attention issue. Second, it would be worthwhile to balance the Theta amplitude in the front part of the brain. This would serve two purposes. The first is that it would help reduce the emotional volatility of this child. This would benefit the child not only in the context of being more emotionally grounded but also reducing his tendency to invite bullying and rejection from his peers because of his emotional sensitivities. Third, balancing the front part of the brain always helps in terms of cognitive efficiency.

Getting the bullying situation under control is no easy matter in very many circumstances. Schools have great difficulty controlling these conditions, or worse, often they simply turn a blind eye to the bullying. We have heard of circumstances in which the victim of bullying is the child who was pulled out of a classroom, or off the playground, because it was easier to isolate the victim than to deal with the bully. Nonetheless, we advise parents to bring these issues to the attention of the school staff to determine what the situation actually is and to work out a strategy for dealing with the problem. Often the parents of the bully are in denial and are not very helpful, either.

Encouraging dialogue with the child is paramount in detection of bullying as well as amelioration of the negative impact of bullying, and in particular cyber bullying. It is interesting to note that in the study discussed earlier the negative effects of cyber bullying were reduced in direct relationship to the number of family dinners the teen reported having each week. This implies that more opportunities for family dialogue provide the opportunity for parents to be able to identify and deal with these troublesome situations.

Table 4.2   Bullied Kids More Likely to Become Psychotic Preteens

- Children who are bullied are more likely to develop psychotic symptoms in early adolescence. Repeated bullying associated with greater risk.
- 6,437 individuals in early adolescence (average age 12.9 years) who were part of the Avon Longitudinal Study of Parents and Children (ALSPAC). Parents completed regular questionnaires about their child's health and development since birth and yearly physical and psychological assessments from the age of 7 years.
- The odds ratio for psychotic symptoms was 1.94 among victims of bullying at ages 8 and/or 10 years and jumped to 4.60 for repeated or severe victimization.
- Victims often less socially skilled and have no or few friends to protect them.
- Monozygotic twin studies: Victimized twin is more likely to develop depression.

Source: Schreier (2009).

The discussion thus far has been focused on children who have come for treatment with a diagnosis of ADHD, and the effects of bullying on their present school situation; however, it is important to note that the effects of bullying can have significant long-term negative effects. Individuals who have been bullied have almost twice the risk of developing psychotic behavior (see Table 4.2). If they have been severely bullied, that ratio increases to about fourfold. Research on identical twins reported by Dr. Louise Arseneault and her colleagues in *Archives of Pediatrics and Adolescent Medicine* (2008) indicates that children who have been bullied have a higher risk of developing depression. We also know that, in addition to any effects on school performance, children who are bullied tend to have fewer friends and hence less protection against bullying. They also tend to be less socially skilled.

It is also important to note that although our focus is on the victim of bullying, bullies also show serious comorbid conditions including poor self-confidence and, later in life, more problems with substance abuse, criminality, and poor achievement. It has been found that the full brunt of childhood bullying may not be realized until adulthood.

Dr. William Copeland and colleagues reported in the *Journal of the American Medical Association* (February 2013) on a study of 1,430 children aged 9, 11, and 13 categorized as either victims only, bullies only, both victims and bullies, or neither. The participants were assessed yearly until age 16 and then periodically until age 26. The results are striking! Victims were about three times more likely to develop an anxiety disorder, panic disorder, and agoraphobia as compared with non-victims. Those who were both bullies and victims were even more at risk. Depending on gender, those in young adulthood were about 5 percent more likely to develop depression and very much more likely to develop agoraphobia, panic disorder, and suicidality as compared with those who were neither victim or bully.

A study of over 4,000 tenth graders by Dr. Laura Bogart and her colleagues, reported in *Pediatrics* (2014), found similar results. Of those with reported poor psychological and general health, 45 percent were presently being bullied and had been bullied in the past; 31 percent were presently being bullied; 12 percent were only bullied in the past; and about 7 percent reported no bullying.

Children living in poverty and those with elevated cultural stressors are more vulnerable to the negative impact of bullying on long-term functioning and well-being. Nevertheless, the results from a study by Dr. Joan Luby and colleagues published in the *Journal of the American Medical Association* (October, 2013) revealed that a nurturing home can lead to lifetime improvements in stress tolerance as reflected in reduced incidence of psychiatric disorders. In fact, brain anatomy is positively affected by nurturance. Dr. Luby et al. report that the reduced size of the hippocampus found in children living in poverty is less likely to be found in children with nurturing parents. Once again, the important lesson is that good parenting can be a game-changer!

FAMILY DYNAMICS

I never cease to be amazed at how easily I fall into the trap of not recognizing an underlying family problem that is either causing or sustaining a child's problems with academic achievement. Part of this, I assume, is my tendency to rely so very heavily on what the brain tells me about difficulties that are neurological in nature.

I also err on the side of accepting parental assessments of the child's condition as being reasonably accurate. The data are quite clear, however, that parents with mood disorders have biased ratings of their children's psychopathology and behavior problems. In a study of 288 parents reporting current depression, mania/hypomania, or mood disorder in remission by Dr. Hagai Maoz and colleagues (*Journal of the American Academy of Child & Adolescent Psychiatry*, 2014), parent mood state significantly affected the accuracy of questionnaire reports regarding their child's symptoms. Parents in manic or hypomanic states were most biased. These researchers also point out that part of the bias may be associated with the disturbed parent having difficulty tolerating their child's behavior and hence see the behavior as more problematic. Some family dynamic issues are not easy to spot. The one that I trip up on routinely is that in which the child must remain symptomatic to satisfy some need within the family.

Jason was a 13-year-old boy that I treated almost 20 years ago. His case is one that always comes back to my mind when I find myself again missing this most fundamental family dynamic problem. Jason was doing okay in school. He had mostly Cs, a smattering of Bs, and the occasional A. His family felt that Jason was not able to achieve at a level consistent with his capabilities; a sentiment to which Jason readily agreed.

We do see many children who are performing adequately in school because fundamentally they are working extra hard to overcome some mild neurological problems associated with the ability to sustain attention. Jason's EEG showed a mild elevation of the Theta/Beta ratio over the central part of the brain. As the reader may recall, this is a condition I call CADD. CADD refers to an attention problem that is associated with hypoactivity of the central regions of the brain causing inattention and often some hyperactivity as well. These children tend to daydream more than other children and it is more difficult for them to sustain attention for any period of time. They can generally improve focus and concentration with increased effort, but it is always a struggle. They tend not to perform well, but frequently perform adequately. Jason's EEG showed the CADD pattern but no other remarkable EEG features that would be associated with academic difficulties.

Jason was the kind of client in whom I felt rather confident that we would be able to help within 10 or 15 sessions, restoring the Theta/Beta ratio to normal levels so he would be able to function more efficiently and with less effort. Jason responded very well to neurotherapeutic treatment. Within eight sessions the Theta/Beta ratio was very close to normative level and within another six sessions he was comfortably below the clinical cut off for the CADD problem.

Jason reported that he felt he was doing much better in school and found homework easier to complete. Jason was using the Omni harmonic (a therapeutic sound that suppresses slow frequency amplitude—Omni is discussed in Chapter Five) every night while he was doing homework and he found it very helpful for sustaining focus and attention. Jason proudly brought in his report card for me to see. His report card had just one C, and the rest were Bs and As!

So was this: a treatment success; get out the "cured" stamp; parents happy as pigs in mud; parents refer many other parents to bring their children for treatment in our clinic; receive a letter from the child a few years later proudly reporting on his successes? I'm afraid not! The next day I received a phone call from Jason's mother asking "Isn't there anything we can do about Jason's ADD? I think we must put him on medication."

It's perfectly clear that I missed something here. And it certainly should have been family therapy time. Jason's parents came in to see me, one at a time; they did not come in together. I should have been more curious about this but made the assumption that schedules did not permit them to come together. It turns out that although the parents were still living in the same house together, separation and divorce had been a topic of conversation for years. From a family dynamic perspective, it appears as though Jason had to remain in some sense problematic, if not disabled, in order to hold the family together. The father recognized this dynamic and felt that there was an unreasonable focus on Jason's condition which he did not feel was markedly problematic. When dealing with the mother about this situation, she admitted that Jason did improve in terms of grades but that he had to work much harder than other children to achieve the same grades. Thus, in her mind, Jason's condition had not really changed all that much. Jason confirmed that his mother focused on his academic difficulties. He said that his mother frequently asked him if he found his work very difficult, if he was getting excessively tired, and she would focus attention on how difficult this was for him. Jason apparently acquiesced to this and would indicate that he felt he was exhausted and working very hard to accomplish his grades.

There are several very important features of this case. First, Jason's EEG assessment did not reflect the family crisis. There was no Alpha blunting at any of the locations nor was there any hyper-vigilance pattern. It could well be that Jason did not feel the brunt of his parents' conflict, in the sense of feeling insecure, or even recognizing that separation of his parents was a decided possibility. In fact, Jason may have felt quite secure given his mother's hovering over him and rewarding his belief that he was working more diligently and overcoming more obstacles than his classmates.

Therapists must be very vigilant about secondary gain. In this situation, both Jason and his mother benefited considerably from Jason's disability. He received significant coddling and attention from his mother and she was able to divert the focus from her troubled marriage to her troubled son. It also provided a means for gaining some degree of control over the marital situation in the sense that the child's well-being should take priority over any other matter; so the looming separation was constantly forestalled. The problem for the therapist is how to get the parents to come in together and sit down and discuss the family issues.

What can the therapist reasonably expect to be able to do about the family strife situation? In Jason's case, dealing with the family dynamic was crucial. Family counseling, of course, would be a recommended option, but for the immediate need to help Jason I suggested third party involvement. In this case, I recommended that a first year university student be hired to spend two hours twice per week with Jason while he was doing his homework. The college student was to lay out strategies for doing homework and to help Jason in terms of planning and organizing his homework time. The college student checked Jason's progress, often on a daily phone-in basis and during the two time periods when he was present with Jason.

This procedure worked rather well for Jason but it did not address the principal issue of the marital conflict. I referred the family to a colleague who is a specialist in family and marital situations but, as I understand, this did not work out well and the family separated. I did learn later that Jason did well in high school and went on to university. One can imagine that this was a situation in which Jason could well have been medicated to sustain a marriage that was in trouble.

Another example of this problem is a family whom we shall call the Kellys. As I have maintained throughout this book, we often find children who are medicated because teachers and/or parents cannot tolerate normal children's behavior. We have a corollary metaphor in which children are often medicated because of intolerable family situations. The case of Jason is one example but a more dramatic illustration of this situation is that of the Kelly's.

Mrs. Kelly brought in her two children, Jane who was seven years of age and Martin who was nine years of age, for treatment of what her family physician thought was ADD with both children. Fortunately for Mrs. Kelly, her family physician was strongly opposed to medicating children for ADHD, unless absolutely necessary. It may well have been that this vigilant physician was suspicious that the problem with the children resided in problems with the family and that medicating this problem would be totally inappropriate. The raw intake data shows the remarkable prescience of the ClinicalQ evaluation, again emphasizing the fact that "the brain tells us everything" we need to know to responsibly treat these complex conditions.

Figure 4.4   ClinicalQ of seven-year-old Jane

CLINICALQ SUMMARY

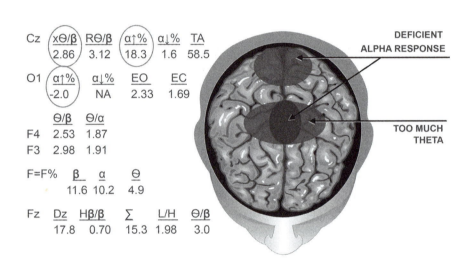

Figure 4.4 shows the initial intake clinical EEG assessment of Jane. Although Jane's EEG shows the feature associated with ADHD (Theta/Beta ratio of 2.86 at location Cz), the feature of particular concern is the blunting of the Alpha response at both locations Cz and O1 (circled numbers—increase in Alpha should be at least 30 percent at location Cz and at least 50 percent at location O1). As the data show, the Alpha response was 18.3 percent at Cz and slightly negative at location O1. These are the markers for exposure to severe emotional stress. One EEG feature we often find with children who have severe attention problems is that they show the trauma marker. It is possible that the trauma is associated with fear of failure and humiliation in school associated with their attention and/or learning problems. However, whenever we see this pattern in children, we always determine if the child is being exposed to marked emotional stressors. This can

be bullying, it could be family strife, or it could be some form of abuse. So in addition to neurotherapeutic treatment for the ADHD, we have to determine the cause of the Alpha blunting.

Mrs. Kelly had brought in both of her children at the same time for back-to-back appointments for the brain assessment. As we can see in Figure 4.5, Martin's EEG looked remarkably similar to Jane's. Both had the marker for ADHD (Theta/Beta ratio of 2.98 at location Cz). In addition, both had markers for exposure to severe emotional stressors. The Alpha blunting was in both locations Cz and O1 (Alpha response of zero at Cz and 39.6% at O1), just as with Jane.

Figure 4.5   ClinicalQ of nine-year-old Martin

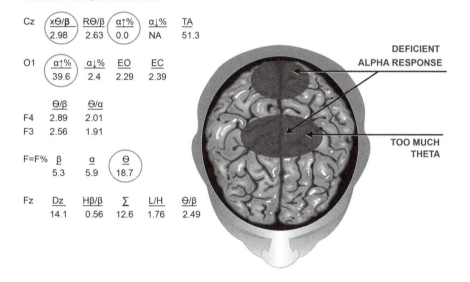

CLINICALQ SUMMARY

Cz	xΘ/β	RΘ/β	α↑%	α↓%	TA
	2.98	2.63	0.0	NA	51.3

O1	α↑%	α↓%	EO	EC
	39.6	2.4	2.29	2.39

	Θ/β	Θ/α
F4	2.89	2.01
F3	2.56	1.91

F=F%	β	α	Θ
	5.3	5.9	18.7

Fz	Dz	Hβ/β	Σ	L/H	Θ/β
	14.1	0.56	12.6	1.76	2.49

DEFICIENT ALPHA RESPONSE

TOO MUCH THETA

There are several important issues to consider here. First, given that we were seeing this marker with both children, it is possible that we were dealing with a genetic factor. Although Alpha blunting is highly correlated with exposure to severe emotional stressors, nonetheless, although rare, we do find it in situations in which there is no apparent present or historical exposure to emotional trauma. The second issue is how we would approach the mother in a manner that was not going to make her bolt from the therapeutic situation or make her severely distraught about her children's well-being. If there is no context in which this parent is aware of severe emotional stress, this kind of information can be clearly distressing. Parents immediately think about bullying, sexual predators, and other forms of abuse to which children might be exposed. It is extraordinarily important for the therapist to be able to deal with this situation in a manner that is rational and systematic.

The third issue is that health care providers have an obligation to report to the authorities any potential harm to a child. However, we had no direct evidence of this other than the EEG data. Recognizing that the parent may be the perpetrator, careful and prudent probing of the parent regarding the various conditions under which the emotional stress may occur, or have occurred, is required.

When I broached the subject of the children showing signs of being exposed to severe emotional stress, Mrs. Kelly broke down and admitted that there were severe problems in the family. According to Mrs. Kelly, her husband vacillated between severe depression and severe emotional abuse. He "flew off the handle" with minimal provocation, was heavily medicated, and she felt that the children were severely disturbed by her husband's behavior. Mrs. Kelly agreed to let me measure her brain wave activity. Her ClinicalQ is shown in Figure 4.6.

Figure 4.6   Mrs. Kelly's ClinicalQ

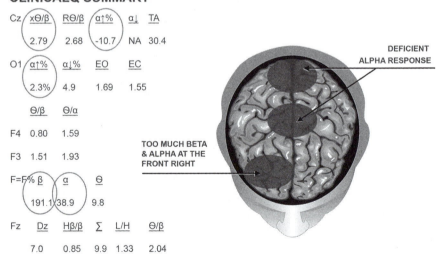

As can be seen in the figure, Mrs. Kelly's EEG shows the marker for exposure to severe emotional stress, just as her children's did. Her brain assessment also shows mild markers for problems with attention, as did her children's, so she is the likely source of the ADD markers that we find in her children. There are several other features of Mrs. Kelly's EEG that are important to note. The first is that she has a major marker for predisposition to depressed mood states; the amplitude of Beta activity is markedly greater (191.1%) in the right prefrontal cortex relative to the left. Regardless of whether Mrs. Kelly's depression contributed to the family dynamic issue or whether it was the result of her exposure to the abusive behavior of her husband, children whose mother is severely depressed are profoundly more likely to have emotional behavior problems.

The second feature in Mrs. Kelly's ClinicalQ is that there is a marked elevation of Alpha amplitude in the right prefrontal cortex relative to the left. In children, we find this imbalance is often associated with oppositional and defiant behavior. In adult populations, we often find this disparity with individuals who are going through severe interpersonal problems such as marital discord, divorce, conflict in the workplace, and so forth.

It seemed obvious that we were dealing with a family in crisis. Both of the children and Mrs. Kelly showed markers for exposure to severe emotional stress (the blunted Alpha trauma markers). Mrs. Kelly showed a major marker for predisposition to depressed mood states and, on her intake self-report assessment, she described herself as being one who falls into depression easily. Mrs. Kelly's description of her children's behavior, like-wise, suggested that these children have some emotional difficulties. She described Jane as easily upset, quick to anger, and unable to engage in cooperative play because she always must win. The latter condition, a child who must always win or they will refuse to play, is a cardinal marker for children who feel insecure and have negative self-regard. This is a charac-teristic often found with adopted children.

Mrs. Kelly described Martin as being very anxious and unresponsive to others' feelings and, importantly, she described him as having behaviors associated with Internet addiction (IA; addiction to video games). This is an extraordinarily serious problem that is largely unrecognized by parents. Although both children showed the neurological pattern associated with CADD, the central problems were emotional and appear to have resulted from family strife as opposed to being associated with ADD. It is, of course, very likely that the ADD was contributing to the family strife. Such children require more assistance and more monitoring to complete their homework assignments and they are usually experiencing difficulties in school, which puts further pressure on the family.

Our ability to diagnose the problem with the Kelly children as being primarily a problem with family strife testifies to the remarkable facility of the EEG as a diagnostic instrument. Without any input from the parents, we were able to determine that family difficulties were giving rise to the problems that were affecting the children. Recall, the children were brought in for treatment because of difficulties in school. The assumption was that the children had some form of ADHD or other learning problem. This testifies to the accuracy of the EEG diagnostic procedure. Most importantly, however, it points out that other therapeutic strategies must be put in place to assist this family. Changing the neurology of the situation is important, but it is a minor component associated with the treatment of these children. It is extremely important to understand that family therapy and treatment of the parents will be equally as important as any kind of neurological work that we might do with the children.

We were most fortunate that Mr. Kelly not only recognized that he had serious problems but also recognized and acknowledged that his behavior was likely to be seriously affecting family functioning in a negative way. He further admitted that he thought his psychological problems were very likely interfering with the children's ability to perform efficiently in school. Mr. Kelly willingly came in for the ClinicalQ assessment, the results of which are shown in Figure 4.7.

Mr. Kelly described himself as follows: "I fly off the handle at minor problems. I'm anxious, depressed, and fatigued. I am on major medications

Figure 4.7   Mr. Kelly's ClinicalQ

CLINICALQ SUMMARY

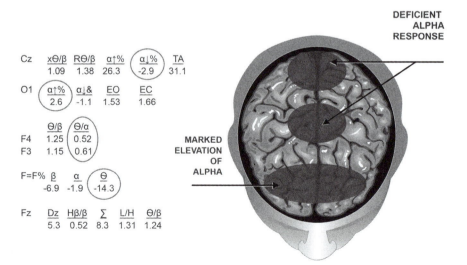

including Wellbutrin, Cipralex, and Ativan that are not very effective. And I've been on other mixes of medications, all of which may have helped somewhat, but eventually lost their effectiveness. I know that my behavior has seriously affected my marriage, my children, and my wife."

Although this situation was severe and complex, I am really tempted to take out the "Cured" stamp at this point! Whenever one has clients who are willing to present themselves for treatment, are open and candid about their problems and their potential influence on other individuals, the prognosis is extraordinarily good for a favorable outcome. There will still be challenges in dealing with this situation, of course. The challenges are not only neurological but behavioral in nature. Martin, for example, had developed a dependency on video games, which provided an escape and stimulation for him and it would be very difficult to wean him from this addictive behavior.

Mr. Kelly had a long history of dysregulated behavior and a long history of being medicated. Titrating him off the medications would be a challenge. Nonetheless, given the data that we had on the neurological condition of each family member and the willingness of both parents to be candid about their condition and enthusiastic about presenting themselves for treatment, the prognosis bodes well for positive outcome.

Mr. Kelly's ClinicalQ indicated a number of anomalies that were interacting and exacerbating each other. That is, they were synergic in a negative sense. Mr. Kelly did not have the marker for the form of ADHD that the children showed and, to some extent, Mrs. Kelly also showed. That form of ADHD is characterized by elevated slow frequency, primarily over the central part of the brain. However, Mr. Kelly did have an ADHD condition and a particularly nasty form, at that. He had marked elevation of Alpha amplitude in the front part of the brain (locations F3 and F4). The reader may recall from Chapter Two the details associated with the high frontal Alpha form of ADHD. The high frontal Alpha form of ADHD is characterized by problems with planning, organizing, sequencing, and following through on things. However, more importantly in this case, the high amplitude frontal Alpha was associated with emotional dysregulation. These individuals can have marked emotional volatility, problems with emotional impulse control, and difficulty sustaining emotional stability. Clients with this neurological condition are often diagnosed with Bipolar Disorder, Personality Disorder, and anxiety disorders in addition to ADHD.

Mr. Kelly also has a mild marker for depressed mood states in which the amplitude of slow frequency Theta is greater in the left front part of the brain as opposed to the right. The reader may recall that predisposition to depression involves a number of conditions that result in the right prefrontal cortex being more active (aroused) than the left. Slow frequency (Theta) amplitude was greater in the left relative to the right in Mr. Kelly's situation. When slow frequency amplitude is greater in the left relative to the right, then the right frontal cortex will be more active than the left, a cardinal marker for depression.

Mr. Kelly had a few other situations that were giving rise to some difficulty. There was a deficiency of slow frequency amplitude relative to fast frequency amplitude (the Theta/Beta ratio) in the occipital region of the brain. Low ratio of the strength of Theta relative to Beta is associated with poor stress tolerance, predisposition to anxiety, sleep quality problems, fatigue, and often leads to self-medicating behavior such as excessive use of alcohol or prescription medications. Mr. Kelly's description of himself included many of these issues. He described himself as "flying off the handle" at minor provocation and being anxious, depressed, and fatigued. Although individuals with low Theta/Beta ratios in the occipital region of the brain have a predisposition for self-medicating behavior, Mr. Kelly denied that he had any difficulty with alcohol. His wife substantiated this. He did comment, however, that he had a very long history of use of prescription medications.

Finally, we note that Mr. Kelly also had the marker for exposure to severe emotional stress. It is not an uncommon finding that the individual whose behavior is the fundamental cause of strife in the family also shows a marker for emotional trauma. It is difficult to know whether Mr. Kelly's trauma markers were associated with his present situation (family in turmoil) or whether this was an historical condition. Mr. Kelly's emotional difficulties may be associated not only with neurological conditions but also with the fact that he had been exposed to severe emotional trauma earlier in his life. Mr. Kelly did admit that he came from an extraordinarily violent household. During his early childhood, he lived in a constant state of fear and anxiety. Hence, it is not unlikely that Mr. Kelly's trauma markers were associated with childhood exposure to severe stress whereas the markers we found in the brain assessments of the children and Mrs. Kelly reflect strife within the family, caused largely by Mr. Kelly's behavior.

Fortunately, from a neurological perspective, it does not matter what the origin of trauma is or when it occurred. As I like to say, "Neurotherapy is the most efficient psychotherapy on the planet." By releasing the blunted Alpha neurotherapeutically, clients often experience trauma releases in which the emotional significance of past traumatic events emerge. These emotional releases may occur during the neurotherapy sessions or shortly thereafter. The releases are usually of short duration and clients usually report emerging from these releases in states of profound emotional quiescence.

The emotional releases associated with the neurological changes in Alpha amplitude frequently occur in sleep. Provided the client has adequate REM sleep (rapid eye movement sleep), the emotional release associated with the neurological change is accomplished during sleep. As discussed in Chapter Three, the reason we focus on the client's sleep architecture quality is so that their "resident psychotherapist" is functioning efficiently. Individuals who were going through the Alpha release often report periods of intense dreaming related to previous emotionally distressing events.

We know that REM sleep is important in terms of integration of what has happened during the day. This is the time during sleep when the brain "files" what has been learned. Without adequate REM sleep, the retention of learned material can be very inefficient. We treat many students who report on their intake questionnaire that they cannot remember what they spend hours studying. Inevitably, they have deficient REM sleep. REM is also critical for processing the emotional experiences that occurred during the day. In other words, it is the brain's psychotherapy. We need about two hours of REM sleep every night to keep ourselves in decent emotional shape and to integrate what we have learned during the day.

When we release the blunted Alpha, the trauma release can occur in many different ways. There can be an increase in dream activity in which the traumatic content is processed, usually in metaphor form. It can occur by having the emotional content "on the front burner," as we say, in which a person is mindful of the emotional historical event for a day or so. It can occur much more intensely in the form of an emotional abreaction in which the client is overwhelmed with the emotions associated with the traumatic event. This is very similar to the flashback in Post-traumatic Stress Disorder in which the individual relives the traumatic emotional event. In general, emotional reactions associated with Alpha release tend to be of minor intensity because the brain has been prepared to process the emotional content efficiently.

It is important to keep in mind that trauma processing does not mean that one is going to forget about the events. What it means is that the meaning of the emotional content changes. The individual sees it in a different perspective and/or the content becomes less relevant because the context changes. For example, a child that shows a trauma marker because of a present emotionally frightening situation, such as poor academic performance, may respond differently when assured of an emotionally secure home environment that is independent of academic performance. And we are all blessed because we are hardwired to have poor recall of pain and discomfort associated with events provided they are not so severe that we need to block the emotional content by blunting the Alpha response.

EMOTIONAL AND BEHAVIORAL DISORDERS IN CHILDREN

Children are often brought in for treatment for an attention deficit disorder when it turns out that the child has emotional and/or behavioral problems that are causing the problem with attention and focus. Of course, we must recognize that this is bidirectional. That is, children who have neurologically based attention deficit problems may develop emotional and/or behavioral problems because of the ADD. These children often feel insecure, unsupported, emotionally distraught, deficient, and just plain stupid because they recognize that they are struggling in school whereas their peers appear to be doing quite well, without comparable struggles.

Whenever a child feels deficient, behavioral problems have a high probability of occurrence. Basically, a child finds it less threatening to be considered a behavioral problem than to be considered stupid. They also tend to quit. Again, it is easier for the child to deal with being considered a person who will not do something as opposed to a person who cannot do something. Children can change the emotional climate by becoming a behavioral problem in school. And classmates may give this child attention for disruptive behavior so that the child is able to limit the emotional pain of feeling stupid.

The child with emotional difficulties, associated with any number of causes, is very likely to have problems with sustaining focus and attention. This can exacerbate the very emotional problem that gave rise to the situation in the first place. So, to repeat, it is a bidirectional condition.

The research on emotional and behavioral problems in children reveals some very interesting data; some of these issues are shown in Table 4.3. Children with emotional behavior problems seem to be more likely to fall between the cracks and not receive an adequate diagnosis and early intervention. It is also apparent that this is not a trivial number of children in that it accounts for about 13 percent of the child population as reported by Dr. Patricia Pastor and her colleagues in the *Center for Disease Control and Prevention, National Center for Health Statistics Report* (2012). These children are less likely to have personal health care providers, less likely to have an early diagnosis and intervention, and most importantly, less likely to have an individual who is coordinating treatment. I call this the "quarterback problem." We see this routinely in the field of neurotherapy. Clients will come for treatment but it turns out that they are also under treatment with a number of other professionals, most of whom appear unaware that other individuals are also treating their client. The client may be receiving individual psychotherapy from a counselor, seeing a psychiatrist for psychotropic medication, seeing a family physician who may be medicating for sleep or anxiety complaints, and may come to a neurotherapist for brain wave biofeedback. Situations such as these have failure written all over them. In my clinic, I insist that I have permission to speak with everybody else who is treating the client. All persons treating a client must be aware of what everyone else is doing and there should be a quarterback who is running and managing treatment. I do not care who the quarterback is provided there is somebody who is managing the entire treatment program.

Table 4.3   Emotional/Behavioral Disorders (EB)

17 Years and Under

- 13 percent of children have special health care needs
- EB least likely to receive care and support
- EB not diagnosed early
- EB require treatment more difficult to access
- Do not have well defined treatments for EB
- Comorbid conditions common
- EB require multidisciplinary treatment—difficult to coordinate, poor interdisciplinary understanding and support (the quarterback problem)

In the case of children with emotional/behavioral difficulties, the quarterback problem is paramount. This is particularly problematic because the treatments for emotional and behavioral problems in children are not well-defined. There are many ways of trying to deal with this, ranging from trying to sedate the behavior pharmaceutically to stringent behavioral programs for controlling negative behavior.

This is precisely the circumstance in which neurotherapy should be considered treatment of choice. The ClinicalQ assessment identifies the neurological conditions causing or exacerbating the emotional and behavioral problems. Further, the ClinicalQ assessment helps us to distinguish those conditions that are neurological from those that are experiential, just as we saw in the case of the Kelly family.

These conditions are extremely complex. On the one hand, children may have emotional and behavioral problems because of some imbalances in the frontal areas of the brain that give rise to emotional volatility, impulse control problems, predisposition to depressed or anxious mood states, and problems with social skill acquisition. On the other hand, children may have emotional problems because of neurological conditions associated with attention deficit disorders and/or learning disorders. As previously noted, these learning disorders can give rise to the child feeling stupid, being bullied, or feeling that parents are disappointed. In short, the child may develop the core emotional belief of self-loathing. And, that is the potential tragedy!

It is also important to keep in mind that after a traumatic brain injury a child's cognitive-executive functioning may recover after a year or so, yet impairments in social functioning may continue for much longer periods of time. This impaired social functioning can impede social development resulting in long-term emotional/behavioral problems as described above. As Dr. Keith Yeates and his colleagues discussed in their article published in *Psychological Bulletin* (2007), the relationship between TBI and a child's social and emotional problems may be overlooked because the cognitive impairments appear to have resolved.

One of the factors associated with emotional and behavioral problems in children, as noted in Table 4.3, is the high level of comorbidity. Children with emotional and behavioral problems often have many other problematic conditions. Table 4.4 lists some of the comorbid conditions that are routinely found in children presenting with emotional and behavioral problems.

Table 4.4   ADHD Comorbidity with Emotional/Behavioral Disorders

- 33% Anxiety and/or Depression
- 20–25% Learning or Language Disorder
- 50% Conduct Disorder
- 70% ADHD will have at least one other mental health or learning disorder during lifetime

Source: ADHD Parents Medication Guide (2013).

As indicated in Table 4.4, we note that about 25 percent of these children are diagnosed with learning disorders and more than 50 percent are diagnosed with a conduct disorder. We also see that 33 percent are diagnosed with anxiety and/or depression conditions. In short, from a neurotherapeutic perspective, the comorbidity picture is simply part of the entire emotional/behavioral disorder complex. In our clinic, we see a great many children who come in with diagnoses of learning, attention, or oppositional disorders whose problems in the school environment turn out to be emotional in nature as opposed to any neurological condition associated with compromises in their ability to learn or pay attention. Again, the Kelly family is a good example of how these circumstances can be extraordinarily complex.

The power of neurotherapy is that it helps us disentangle all of this so that we are treating the right conditions, whether they are neurological, social, behavioral, or emotional in nature.

Children with a physical disorder present a slightly different problem. These children are very likely to place the family under some financial, emotional, and time constraints which present a special family burden. The major factor here is whether the parents, grandparents, and siblings consider the physical condition to be a burden. As indicated in Table 4.5, children with emotional/behavioral problems are more likely to have a family member who considers their physical condition to be a burden. This burden can be financial or restriction of the family member's ability to work, or requiring a family member to devote a significant amount of time to caring for the physically challenged child.

Table 4.5   Family Burden Related to Child's Health Problems

Child with Emotional/Behavioral Disorder (EB) more likely to have family member who

- Experience financial problem related to child's health
- Reduced or stopped work because of child's health
- Spent 11 or more hours/week providing or coordinating care
- EB less likely to have personal physician

Table 4.6   Emotional/Behavioral Consequences of Chronic Illness

- Internalizing: depression, withdrawal. More likely from pain and limiting disorders such as arthritis, asthma, diabetes
- Externalizing: aggression. More likely when disorder affects brain regulation; e.g., epilepsy.

Source: Pinquart and Shen (2011).

It is also useful to note, as pointed out in Table 4.6, that the nature of the physical disorder can influence the type of emotional/behavioral disorder of the child. Disorders that are more likely to limit physical activity, such as arthritis and asthma, are more likely to give rise to depression and withdrawal. Disorders that affect brain regulation, such as seizure disorders, are more likely to give rise to aggression.

Recall the case of Clarita discussed in the Chapter Three. Clarita had an imbalance in the frontal cortex of the brain. The right side had significantly stronger Theta than the left side. This condition is associated with emotional dysregulation. Imbalances of this nature are often found with clients diagnosed with Histrionic Personality Disorder (HPD), as was the case with Clarita. This genetic condition usually does not manifest in childhood as histrionics but more likely as oppositional and defiant behavior. The imbalance often also affects learning efficiency so Clarita would likely experience difficulties in school. Clarita, as you may recall, denied any problems in her early school experience but found that she struggled in university. Clarita's case exemplifies the therapeutic power of the ClinicalQ. Clarita could have been shouldered with any number of diagnostic labels including, ADHD, ODD, General Anxiety Disorder (GAD), HPD, and Pervasive Developmental Disorder (Not Otherwise Specified) [PDD (NOD)]. It would likely be later in life before Clarita would manifest the behaviors associated with the histrionic personality disorder diagnosis that she reported on the intake questionnaire when she came to the clinic. And, as we saw with the Kelly family, Clarita's emotional dysregulation would likely affect her entire family.

THE EMOTIONAL CLIMATE OF THE FAMILY

As the case of the Kelly family exemplified, the emotional climate of the family is critical to the well-being of the child. In that case, Mr. Kelly's emotional dysregulation problems were causing significant difficulty in the family which resulted in some behavioral, emotional, and learning problems with his two children. Although Mr. Kelly's children did have neurological markers for an attention deficit issue, nonetheless, the major factor associated with the emotional and behavioral problems of these children was the emotional climate of the family.

Of course, many forms of emotional dysregulation of the parent(s) can impact substantially upon the emotional health of the child. Parents who are highly critical can discourage children from engaging in any endeavor, whether it is schoolwork, sports, or any other creative activities. For example, individuals who are personality disordered are often highly critical of others. This can be a defensive emotional state motivated by severely negative core emotional beliefs about themselves. Children who are severely physically abused by a parent frequently develop emotional beliefs about themselves that they are unworthy and unlovable. These negative core emotional beliefs can evolve into self-loathing. These individuals can later manifest personality disorders that in turn may include defensive symptoms, such as hypercritical interpersonal behavior. Parents who are quick to anger, such as Mr. Kelly, can create an environment in which the child does not feel safe. Children who do not feel safe are less likely to express their emotional sentiments other than those associated with fear. They may also be very cautious about engaging in any activities that can give rise to parental anger.

One problem that we see routinely with children who are brought into our clinic is that of parental depression. As the data shown in Table 4.7 indicate, children who are diagnosed with emotional and/or behavioral problems are much more likely to come from families in which one or both parents are depressed. The risk of emotional and behavioral problems increases when either parent is depressed, more prominently if the mother is depressed, and has the highest occurrence when both parents are depressed. It is also interesting to note, as pointed out in Table 4.8, that although we tend to identify postpartum depression with the mother, about 10 percent of fathers also experience postpartum depression.

Table 4.7   Risk for Emotional/Behavioral Disorders Associated with Parental Depression

6%—neither parent depressed
19%—mother depressed
11%—father depressed
23%—both parents depressed

Source: Weitzman et al. (2011).

Table 4.8   Parental Post-Partum Depression

• Mother: 10–30%
• Father: 10%

Source: Paulson and Bazemore (2010).

It is interesting to note that one sees a very similar pattern of familial influence with chronic pain in children. As shown in Table 4.9, a child is more than twice as likely to develop a chronic pain condition if both parents have a similar condition. The child is almost twice as likely to develop such a condition if in a single parent household with a parent with chronic pain. This ratio is modulated a bit if the child is in a two-parent household but one parent does not have a chronic pain condition.

Table 4.9   Familial Influence on Child's Chronic Pain Syndrome

N=5,370; 13–18 Years of Age	
Parental Pain	**Odds Ratio**
One in Couple	1.5
Both in Couple	2.3
Single Mother	1.9
Single Father	1.8

Source: Hoftun et al. (2012, November).

FATHER ABSENT HOUSEHOLDS

The numbers are staggering. In the United States, one third of children live in homes with the father absent. In general, children in these homes do less well than those with the father present. They have more problems in school, have more emotional/behavioral problems, and are more prone to addictive behaviors. There are many hypotheses about the social/emotional factors that may be the cause of these negative effects.

But, what about the neurology? Research from McGill University, published in the journal *Cerebral Cortex* (2013), by Dr. Gabriella Gobb and her colleague suggests that the absence of the father during critical developmental phases may actually result in physical changes in the brain. Children from father absent households have increased risk for deviant behavior, attention and learning problems, and, for girls in particular, increased risk for substance abuse.

The McGill researchers used an animal model for studying the effects on brain functioning of father absence. A specific strain of mice that is monogamous and raise their offspring together were used as subjects. Those raised with father absent showed abnormal social interactions and were more aggressive than those raised by both parents. The female pups also showed greater sensitivity to the stimulant drug amphetamine. Further, these anomalies were associated with defects in the prefrontal cortex, an area of the brain associated with social and cognitive activity.

These are very intriguing findings. As we have discussed previously, negative social experiences can result in blunting of the Alpha response (the trauma markers), but appear to also often result in an imbalance in the frontal regions of the brain with Alpha having greater amplitude in the right relative to the left. It is also worth keeping in mind that unavailability of a parent can be the result of serious depression as well as physical absence.

EMOTIONAL CLIMATE OF THE FAMILY:
PRAISE AND EXPECTATIONS

We have examined a variety of the conditions that affect a child's ability to attend and learn in school. We have discussed ADD, ADHD, ASD, ODD, PDD (NOS), OCD, as well as conditions less likely to be identified with an acronym. In this section, I would like to broaden our discussion of family dynamics that can negatively affect children's academic (and social) performance. These include GSIM (born with Golden Spoon In Mouth), NPFS (expects Nobel Prize For Showering), TSTC (Too Sensitive To Compete), TATF (Tough Act To Follow), Gifted, TSTL (Too Sensitive To Learn), MCTJ (My Child The Jokester), MSCISRS (My Special Child Is So Really Special), and the list goes on.

I was told by an Irish client that "in the old country" they had a saying: "Clogs to Clogs" in three generations. The implication was that the third generation could not live up to the expectations of the parent who had clawed his or her way out of poverty. We see many such clients in the clinic; children with very successful parents who are tainted by the parents' success. They often feel entitled. They expect special treatment, rewards without effort, and the privilege to make effort dependent on feelings rather than necessity. This entitlement state can evolve into loss of interest, motivation, and purpose for meaningful activity.

It can be the reverse, of course, in which parents have hugely unrealistic expectations for the child. The child simply cannot keep up, is exhausted, and develops a severe core emotional belief that they are not good enough. This can look like ADHD in that the child loses interest, refuses to engage, quits, or becomes behaviorally disruptive.

Unrealistic parental expectations, whether explicit or implied, can have devastating effects on children. This often does not manifest until late teens and early college age. A good indicator of this problem is the university parking lot drug dealers. These dealers are not pushing crack cocaine, or ecstasy, or downers. They are dealing in mind excitatory drugs such as Adderall and other stimulants. It has become part of the culture at elite universities that one needs these drugs to be competitive in these high expectation environments. And perhaps the marked elevation in suicides at these universities is a further indictor of the TATF condition. Of course, TATF can result in the child rebelling or just quitting because he or she feels they simply cannot live up to the expectations from their parents and/or the broader community.

This evening as I left the clinic, I saw several office staff trying to get stains out of the waiting room carpeting. A child had been drawing on the carpet with markers and the carpet was a mess. The parent was present and apparently aware of this activity, but was certainly aware when the child and the parent left the waiting room—parent said nothing about the mess on our carpet. I then entered the elevator with a number of adults and one child who pushed every button, forcing the elevator to stop at every floor. Parent did not intervene but simply laughed at the child's behavior.

This is not a book on parenting, so, we do not need to belabor this other than to point out that many children brought in for treatment of attention deficiencies and learning problems have only one very major problem: IP (Incompetent Parenting). Parents, teachers, physicians, psychologists, psychiatrists, school counselors, all have one recommended treatment for IP: Medicate the child!

There are differences among the labels; but the critical element in all of these conditions is structure. Rules are rules; praise is earned; violation of a rule results in a 100 percent credible, instantaneous consequence.

Unconditional love from parents has enormous benefits for the child. They are more secure, have greater achievement in school, have more friends, and even in neurotherapy, they respond more efficiently to treatment. What unconditional love means is the child knows to the bottom of their tiny little hearts that the love of their parents is absolutely independent of their achievements.

Unconditional praise destroys the child! Reward what you want to encourage, and respond instantly to any rule infraction with a VERY MILD but 100 percent credible (an infraction ALWAYS leads to) negative consequence. Keep in mind that you are teaching the child, not punishing the child. Unconditional praise teaches the child that effort is not required. An excellent book on this subject is *NurtureShock* by journalists Po Bronson and Ashley Merryman.

A final note on the emotional climate of the family. As all parents know, the new digital age is markedly affecting the emotional climate of the family. I was reminded of this recently when I observed a family having dinner at a restaurant. There were three generations at the table: young children, the parents of the young children, and an elderly couple who, I assumed, were the grandparents. All the young children were on their cell phones and the parents were both on their cell phones as well. The elderly couple was sitting in silence looking quite sad and dejected.

Perhaps I was reading too much into this observation, but it is interesting that recent data on frequency of family dinners at home has a very therapeutic value for reducing the harm associated with cyber bullying. In a study of almost 19,000 adolescents, almost 20 percent had experienced cyber bullying in the past year. Of that number almost 20 percent reported depression; almost 5 percent reported suicide attempts; and about 6 percent prescription drug abuse. However, these children were also asked "how many days a week they had evening meals with their family" with range of 0 to 7. This study, by Dr. Elgar and colleagues, published in *Pediatrics* (2014), found that the link between cyber bullying and mental health and substance abuse problems was weaker among teens who reported having more family dinners. Family dinner ratings are used as a proxy for family contact and communication suggesting that positive family emotional climate supporting more open emotional communication offers protection for the victimized child. It is also obvious that the parental rule "no cell phones at the dinner table" is sacrosanct!

RELATIONSHIP PROBLEMS

As we saw in the case of the Kelly family, the ClinicalQ can often identify situations that are likely to be extant and of a personal nature. We saw this also in the case of the child that we suspected was exposed to bullying. In that situation, we saw the Alpha blunting that can be associated with severe emotional stress, and some imbalances in the front part of the brain that are often indicative of reactive depression and interpersonal conflict. In adults, we often see patterns in the EEG indicating that the individual may be going through some interpersonal difficulties such as marital discord, divorce, or problems in the workplace.

When dealing with adolescents and young adults, we should keep in mind that the attention and learning difficulties they are experiencing may have been caused by, or exacerbated by, some interpersonal problem. We often see this pattern, which leads us to probe the client to determine if the child is being bullied, either in person or cyber bullied, or having some other interpersonal difficulties. The basic ClinicalQ data for Nadine, a sixteen-year-old female with this pattern, are shown in Figure 4.8a. The topographical representation of these anomalies is shown in Figure 4.8b.

Nadine's case is a perfect example of a child who has a marker for mild attention deficit problems but a very major marker for possible problems of an interpersonal nature. It is our best guess that Nadine is experiencing severe bullying or some problems with her family or, given her age, problems with a boyfriend. This child is sixteen years old. The markers associated with interpersonal strife are highlighted. The brain locations of these markers are shown in Figure 4.8b. First of all, we have the trauma marker at both locations. The Alpha response at CZ, that should be at least

Figure 4.8a   A relationship problem?

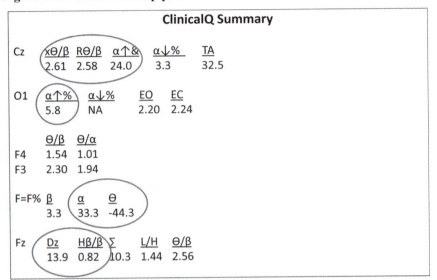

Figure 4.8b   Topographical schematic of Nadine's brain activity

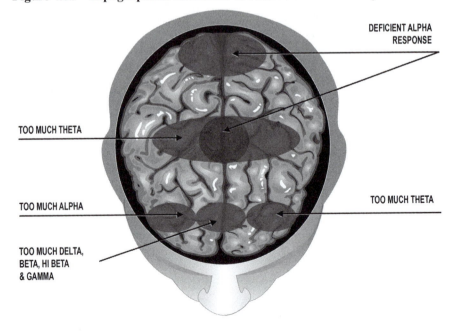

30 percent, is 24 percent. At O1, the Alpha response should be above 50 percent whereas in her case it is only 5.8 percent. In addition to the trauma markers, she has a marker for reactive depression and a marker for some interpersonal issues.

The reactive depression markers are when Theta and/or Alpha amplitude is considerably greater in the left frontal cortex relative to the right. This is often associated with depression that is a response to some condition as opposed to a genetic marker for predisposition to depressed mood states. There have been a number of studies indicating that if you expose a person to conditions that give rise to sadness, such as very sad story, you will get a temporary increase in slow frequency amplitude in the left relative to the right, indicating that the right is more active than the left for that period of time.

The marker suggesting some interpersonal angst is where Alpha amplitude is greater in the right frontal cortex relative to the left. In young children, this pattern is often associated with oppositional and defiant behaviors. And, as we just discussed, may also be associated with father absence during early developmental phases. The child diagnosed with ODD often shows this pattern of elevated right frontal Alpha amplitude. In older children and adults with this pattern, we often find that there is an extant interpersonal situation that is problematic and emotionally distressing. As mentioned several times in this book, we often see this pattern in adults who are going through marital discord of some sort.

The interesting question to ask is if this imbalance, that may be reflective of an oppositional and defiant personality, identifies a person who will inevitably have difficulty in relationships, or is it reflective of the difficulty in the relationship itself that results in this imbalance in the front part of the brain. In either case, this Alpha imbalance suggests that there is likely to be some form of interpersonal angst. The imbalance guides the therapist in probing the client to determine whether there are any interpersonal situations that are exacerbating the condition for which the client is seeking treatment. Nadine was sent in by her parents because of some difficulties in school, and particularly, for attention and focus problems. After questioning the parents, I found out that the situation became considerably more problematic recently, which prompted the parents to encourage Nadine to come in for an evaluation.

I asked Nadine if she was experiencing any difficulties interpersonally; for example, was she having problems with her friends, did she feel like she was being isolated or excluded, was she having problems with a boyfriend, or was she having some difficulties within her family? Nadine indicated surprise that the brain assessment could reveal such problems. It turned out that she was having a lot of difficulty with her boyfriend. Nadine's unhappiness with her relationship had been going on for some period of time and she and her boyfriend broke up recently. I pointed out to Nadine that these kinds of situations can markedly exacerbate a mild problem associated with attention and focus difficulties. I further told Nadine that we would be able to help her with the attention and focus problems but simply reminded her that her emotional state can also cause or intensify problems with focus and attention.

INTERNET ADDICTION

More years ago than I care to admit, I and many other parents inadvertently were exposing our children to the risk of Internet Addiction (IA). In those early days of the computer, when my child said he was going upstairs to his bedroom to play games on his computer, my response to this was very positive and encouraging. I thought, incorrectly it turns out, that the child is learning how to operate a computer and would become versatile and knowledgeable about this new technology. Advance a few decades to when I was a lecturer in psychiatry at Harvard Medical School, and one of my colleagues opened the first IA clinic in North America. Many of us were curious about this, not recognizing the full detrimental effects of addiction to this new technology.

IA is a huge problem. The focus in this book is on children's difficulties in school and whether the child's problems are really ADHD or the result of some other factors. Although IA is a severe problem affecting many adults, our focus here is on children.

At the simplest level, children avoid doing homework because they are addicted to the arousal and stimulation of video games. In addition, they often avoid physical activity and playing with peers because they prefer Internet activities to these alternatives. Aside from the obvious health implications of insufficient physical activity and sleep deprivation, constant exposure to video game stimulation makes children more prone to having difficulty sustaining attention in lower stimulation environments, such as classrooms.

Parents often enable this addiction because video games are an extraordinarily good babysitter. Children will spend hours playing a video game and not require parental supervision or engagement. Although beyond the scope of this book, it is important to note that video game addiction is one of the most serious impediments to successful treatment of any of the autism spectrum disorders. Frazzled parents of autistic children understandably welcome the reprieve provided by the child's absorption into the video game. In a sense, they are codependent to the IA just as the spouse of an alcoholic can be codependent. We are still learning about the full extent of the problem associated with addiction to this new technology. An excellent book covering the full range and complexity of this serious social issue is *i-Minds* (2015) by Dr. Mari Swingle.

Many of the children who are prone to addiction to video games are those who show the markers for elevated slow frequency of the form that we find with common ADD. Frequently, these children will also show a deficiency in slow frequency in the back of the brain associated with problems with stress tolerance. We also often find an imbalance in the frontal cortex with Alpha amplitude being considerably greater in the right relative to the left. The reader may recall that this imbalance is often associated with problems interpersonally or with oppositional and defiant behaviors. It also can be associated with problems with social skills and the ability to interact comfortably with peers. We are still in the infancy stage in terms of understanding the full implications of IA and much research is presently underway to understand the complexities of the situation.

The consequences of IA are listed in Table 4.10. It is obvious that this is a very serious condition that can have severe negative effects on families. The problem is not limited to children and adolescents but affects all ages, social classes, and both genders. For our purposes the focus is on children. Although we find some neurological conditions associated with this and other addictions, a major component of the treatment must be behavioral. As we say, change takes effort, and the parents and the child must be focused on getting the addictive behavior under control. Obviously, the earlier this

Table 4.10   Consequences of Internet Addiction

- Financial debt
- Work/school implications: fired, suspended, penalized, expelled
- Suicidal ideation/attempts/completions
- Lack of meaningful relationships
- Social awkwardness
- Malnourishment
- Poor hygiene
- Family discord
- Lack of spirituality or emotional health
- Failure to fulfill personal responsibilities

pattern of addictive behavior is recognized and dealt with, the more promising the outcome.

Figure 4.9 shows the brain assessment of a fourteen-year-old male child who has a severe IA. This is typical of what we find. There is a marker for the inattentive form of ADHD, a marker for poor stress tolerance, and the imbalance in Alpha that we discussed previously. This pattern, although common, is not the only pattern that we find with the Internet addicted clients. Recent research by Dr. Mari Swingle (*i-Minds*, 2015) has indicated that many forms of neurological dysregulation can be a risk factor for IA. This indicates, as has been repeated often in this book, that we look at what the brain is telling us to direct the treatment as opposed to any one-size-fits all treatments for IA or any other condition, for that matter.

Figure 4.9   ClinicalQ EEG assessment of a child with a severe IA

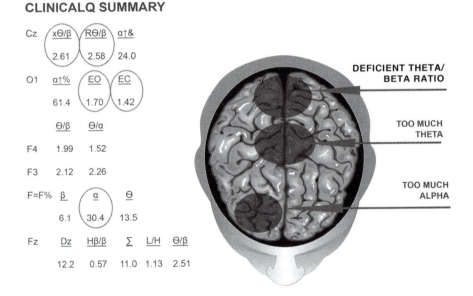

As with any addiction, changing the neurology is only part of the treatment. This child is going to require behavioral modification to help wean off of the excessive involvement with the video games. This can be very challenging. In a sense, it is very similar to an eating disorder. When treating an eating disorder, we cannot simply have the person stop eating. Likewise with IA; because of the reliance on computers and the Internet in schools and in the work environment, some Internet exposure will be absolutely necessary.

Figures 4.10 and 4.11 show the ClinicalQ EEG summaries for an adult male and an adult female with severe IA. Common to both of the adults and the child is the Alpha disparity in the frontal cortex and the deficiency in the Theta/Beta ratio at the back of the brain. The child and the adult female also have the markers for common ADD.

Figure 4.10   ClinicalQ EEG summary for an adult male with severe IA

CLINICALQ SUMMARY

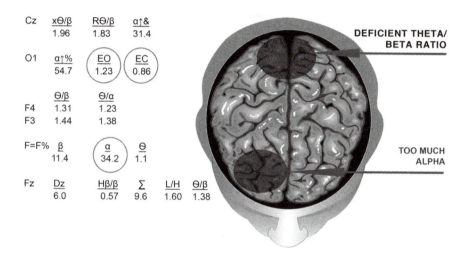

The adult female has the most serious IA that was completely interfering with her work. Her ClinicalQ also shows the most severe conditions, which include a marker for predisposition to depression, mood volatility, and obsessive/compulsive behaviors and a trauma marker (i.e., history of severe emotional stress). So, it is obvious that although there are commonalities in these EEG profiles, each of these clients with IA require individualized treatment specific to the anomalies found in their brain functioning. Clearly, one-size-fits-all treatments are not efficient means for helping these individuals who all share the label "Internet Addiction." It is also obvious that treating the fourteen-year-old child for ADHD is very likely to fail since the cause of the problem is principally the IA. Table 4.11 shows some of the statistics on the apparent prevalence of IA among several groups. The conditions that are indicative of IA are itemized in Table 4.12.

Figure 4.11   ClinicalQ EEG summary for an adult female with severe IA

CLINICALQ SUMMARY

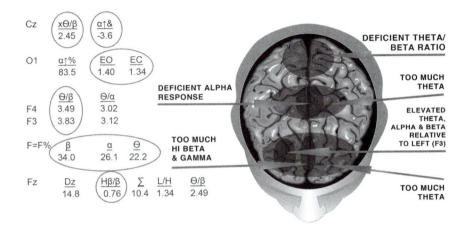

Table 4.11   IA Prevalence

- About 9% of children (8–18 years) show gaming addiction symptoms
- Eighty percent of children game on internet
- IA in general population: 6–14%
- Can be as high as 38% in some groups

Source: Swingle (2015).

Table 4.12   Internet Addiction Test (IAT) Items

- School or work performance suffers
- Defensive or secretive about time on and/or what is done online
- Block out thoughts with online use or anticipated use
- Fear that life without Internet boring, empty, joyless
- Snap, yell, or act annoyed if Internet interrupted by others
- Sleep loss associated with late night Internet use
- Fantasize about Internet use
- Try and fail to cut down on use of Internet
- Choose Internet over going out with others
- Feel depressed, moody, or anxious when offline, which goes away online
- Stay online longer than intended
- Prefer excitement of Internet to intimacy with partner
- Others complain about time online

In general, children who are more prone to addiction to video games are those who show elevated slow frequency amplitude of the form that we find with common ADD. These children also frequently show a deficiency in slow frequency amplitude in the back of the brain associated with poor stress tolerance. We also often find an imbalance in the frontal cortex with Alpha amplitude being considerably greater in the right relative to the left. The reader will recall that this imbalance is often associated with interpersonal problems such as poor social skills or problems with oppositional and defiant behaviors. It also can be associated with problems with social skills resulting in the inability to interact comfortably with peers. We are still in the infancy stage in terms of understanding the full implications of IA and much research is presently underway to understand the complexities of the situation.

The technology keeps changing so that the IA risk factors are constantly changing. We really do not have any understanding of the potential impact of the texting revolution that is taking place in which individuals are in constant written contact with a number of their peers. Does this have the potential to manifest as another form of IA? Will it interfere with the learning of social skills? How will it relate to the development, manifestation, or treatment of the social phobias? Will children learn to prefer Internet contact over face-to-face interaction with friends and peers?

CASE EXAMPLE: A CHILD IN CRISIS

Whenever we see brain wave data such as that shown in Figures 4.12 and 4.13, it is certain that we have a child in crisis. And the essential worrisome features of this ClinicalQ include: blunted Alpha response at both Cz and O1; marked deficiency in the Theta/Beta ratio at O1; marked elevation of Beta in the front part of the brain; marked elevation of high frequency amplitude at Fz; and elevated Delta at Fz. This child is also extraordinarily bright.

Looking at these conditions sequentially, we find that the blunted Alpha at both CZ and O1 are indicative of exposure to severe emotional stressors. So first we must probe to determine just what emotional stressors this child is being, or has been, exposed to. We also note that there is a marked deficiency in the Theta/Beta ratio at the back of the brain, likely a genetic condition, which is a predisposition to poor stress tolerance, anxiety, self-medicating behavior, and poor sleep quality. Deficient Theta/Beta ratio at O1 is also often associated with problems with staying focused because of racing thoughts.

In the frontal regions of the brain, we see again marked elevation of Beta amplitude, typically found in the highly anxious children. We also see insufficient Alpha amplitude relative to Beta and Theta, which is a condition often associated with hypervigilance, found in clients who have been exposed to severe emotional stressors.

At the frontal midline, location Fz, we find that the amplitude of both Beta and Gamma are markedly elevated, which is a marker for fretting. This child has summated high frequency amplitude (i.e., the amplitude of both Beta and Gamma is 42.6 which is markedly above the normative range, which is below 15). The ratio of Beta to Gamma amplitude is 1.26, which is the marker for obsessive thought processes. Finally, we see that Delta

Figure 4.12   A Child in crisis—ClinicalQ at locations Cz, O1, F3 and F4, and Fz

CZ	Values	%Change
EO Alpha	13.44	
EC Alpha	16.00	
Percent change EO to EC Alpha > 30%		19.06%
EO Alpha Recovery	12.58	
% difference EO Alpha from initial EO after EC		−6.85%
Theta Amplitude EO	26.31	
Beta Amplitude EO	17.16	
EO Theta/Beta < 2.2	1.54	
Theta Amplitude Under Task (UT)	23.75	
Beta Amplitude UT	15.91	
UT Theta/Beta	1.50	

O1	Values	%Change
Alpha EO	11.40	
Alpha EC	15.41	
% Change in Alpha EO to EC >50%		35.12%
EO Alpha Recovery	11.29	
% change EO Alpha to EO Alpha after EC < 25%		−1.03%
Theta Amplitude EO	21.32	
Beta Amplitude EO	22.74	
Theta/Beta EO 1.8 - 2.2	0.95	
Theta Amplitude EC	22.86	
Beta Amplitude EC	20.99	
Theta/Beta EC 1.8 - 2.2	1.09	

F3 and F4	F3	F4	
* F4><F3 Beta <15%	16.93	17.08	0.90%
* F4><F3 Alpha <15%	12.37	12.45	0.64%
* F4><F3 Theta <15%	19.35	20.43	5.57%

FZ	Values
Delta (2 Hz) EC < 9.0	18.01
HiBeta Amplitude	23.92
Beta Amplitude	18.65
HiBeta/Beta .45 - .55	1.27
Sum HiBeta + Beta <15	42.57
LoAlpha Amplitude	6.19
HiAlpha Amplitude	6.82
LoAlpha/HiAlpha 1.0 - 1.5	0.91
Alpha Peak Frequency EC	9.9

amplitude is markedly elevated again over the frontal midline. Although we do not have much firm evidence for this as yet, elevated frontal Delta is frequently seen in children who have been exposed to emotionally traumatic situations and may be a form of emotional numbing.

The reader may recall the case of the Kelly's in which the problems the children were having in school were likely caused by, or at least markedly exacerbated by, the emotional climate at home. Here we have a similar situation in which the child has no markers for any of the attention problems other than the elevated Delta amplitude in the front part of the brain. As mentioned earlier, although we do not have much evidence for this generalization, clinically, we often find elevated Delta in such situations. The elevated Delta amplitude may be associated with emotional numbing or the brain may be fatigued because of the marked elevation in high frequencies associated with high levels of anxiety and stress.

So, how do we help this child? First we have to determine what kind of stressors this child is being exposed to and whether the situation is ongoing.

Figure 4.13   Topographic schematic of brain areas implicated in "child in crisis"

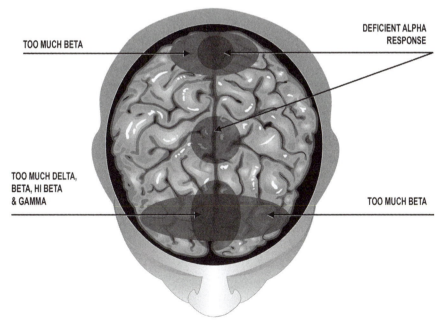

There are a number of possibilities: this child may be exposed to severe bullying, she could be being abused at home, she could be being abused by a neighbor, she may be terrified about a family member's illness; the possibilities are almost endless. We must also be mindful that the trauma may be mild or insignificant by normal standards but is having a very severe impact on this child because of her poor stress tolerance.

The stressors to which this child was being exposed were severe. A cherished grandparent had died within the last few months. One of her parents was recently diagnosed with a terminal illness. The child was not supposed to know about the terminal illness but, of course, these kinds of conditions dramatically affect the emotional climate in the family, regardless of the heroic efforts of parents to try to protect the child.

So, from a psychological perspective, this child's core emotional security was being clearly threatened. She lost a grandparent, a severe emotional event for a child her age. She was also at risk for losing a parent as well. Now, whether or not the child understood that the life of her parent was at risk, we know that children respond markedly to the emotional state of parents. The surviving parent would unquestionably be emotionally removed from the child because of severe depression, anxiety, and fear associated with the impending loss of the partner.

Once the nature of the trauma was determined, other forms of family-oriented therapy were required to help this family deal with the traumatic situation. In terms of what neurotherapy could contribute to the treatment of this child, the focus was on improving stress tolerance and decreasing the emotional fretting and hyper-vigilance. This is a particularly good example of a situation in which neurotherapy played a minor role in terms of correcting some neurological conditions, whereas family and individual counseling played the major role in terms of helping this child through the emotional crisis. The reader will appreciate that treating this child with one-size-fits-all neurotherapy boarders on malpractice.

Before we move on, we must keep in mind that trauma markers must be taken very seriously. Often they are associated with conditions such as those described in the cases we reviewed, including the Kelly's and the most recent case of the child in crisis. In other circumstances, trauma markers can be associated with bullying, being socially rejected, or the child's emotional reaction to doing poorly in school because of an ADHD condition. However, the trauma marker can be associated with child abuse. Hence, when the trauma marker is observed, thorough probing is required to identify the causes and, if necessary, actions must be taken to protect the child.

We also frequently see trauma markers when there are no apparent emotional stressors of any prominent nature. "Trauma" is probably a poor term to use because it always suggests the sensational when, in fact, it can be a cumulative situation of loneliness and despair. A good example of this is the situation of a depressed parent on the emotional state of the child.

We see older adults who often show the trauma marker and when asked about their history of exposure to severe emotional stress, they seem at a loss to recall any such circumstance that would reach the level of "trauma." However, upon reflection, they indicate that their childhood was extremely unpleasant, although not dangerous in any sense. Their home was always secure and they were well cared for. But it turns out that one or both parents were severely depressed and not emotionally available to the child. These adult clients often report that their childhood was characterized by profound loneliness and unhappiness.

We should always keep in mind that trauma markers may be associated with the child being exposed to physical and/or emotional abuse. Parents may not be aware of the abusive situation or they may be responsible for the abuse. The therapeutic and diagnostic power of the ClinicalQ reveals the circumstances in a very rapid and efficient manner. In conventional therapy, determining that a child has been exposed to a severe emotional trauma, or severe emotional stressors, may take many sessions and, in fact, totally elude the therapist.

As I have said routinely throughout this book, the brain tells us everything. However, in addition to telling us everything, it also puts us in a position of responsibility to the child to determine the exact nature of the conditions to which this child is being exposed. Just considering sexual abuse alone, the data are quite sobering. As shown in Table 4.13, many children are exposed to a sexual encounter with an adult. So on average it is prudent to assume that a significant number of children who are seen in therapy have been sexually abused. Table 4.14 also shows that adolescents are likely to have been exposed to at least one potentially emotionally traumatic experience.

Table 4.13   Sexual Abuse Statistics

U.S. Statistics

Report (nonconsensual) sexual encounter with an adult before the age of 18

• Females: 25%
• Males: 16%

Source: Botash (1997).

Table 4. 14   Potentially Traumatic Experiences (PTE)

- From a group of 6,483 teens, 61% reported exposure to at least one PTE in their lifetime, including interpersonal violence such as rape, physical abuse, or witnessing domestic violence, as well as injuries, natural disasters, and the death of a close friend or family member.
- A total of 19% of respondents reported three or more such events.
- Prevalence of PTSD in those exposed to trauma was 4.5%, a rate that approaches that in U.S. adults, and was significantly higher in females (7.3%) than males (2.2%).

Source: McLaughlin (2013, August).

Data from a number of Canadian studies indicate that in 4–11-year-old school children samples, about 15 percent of boys and about 10 percent of girls admit to having bullied another child, although schoolyard observational studies indicate that the frequency between males and females is quite similar. About 5 percent of boys and about 7 percent of girls report having been bullied and a large number admit to being bystanders when bullying is occurring. Interesting data on bullying in Canada can be obtained from the publicsafety.gc.ca website.

Data regarding frequency of child abuse are difficult to obtain but incidence of reports are in the neighborhood of 2 percent. Abuse, of course, is not limited to broken bones and bruises. It includes any circumstance in which the physical and emotional needs of the child are ignored, wantonly or inadvertently.

So, again, from a therapist's point of view, when a trauma marker is observed, we should assume that a sizeable number of the children with these markers have experienced severe emotional stress. Parents may not be reliable sources of information about trauma. They may be unaware of the bullying their child is being exposed to at school.

Parents often underestimate the severity of the emotional impact of an event on the child. A recent example of this was a child I saw who showed the trauma marker. I questioned the parent who was at a loss to identify any emotional stressor that would be of a severe nature. Later, he recalled that his child had sustained an injury in her mouth. Her injury was treated rapidly but was none-the-less traumatic to the child because of a situation she observed in a television program. The child depicted in the television episode sustained what she thought was a similar injury that was life threatening.

And, unfortunately, we also have out-of-touch parents. One situation comes to mind in which, in response to my query about a trauma marker, the father of the child said that there was "nothing that his child had not dealt with." This, of course, is a red-flag response. Upon further questioning, it turned out that the child's uncle had committed suicide a few weeks earlier!

IMMATURITY OR ADHD?

One of my pet peeves is that we are medicating (and "treating") the normal behavior of children. We have simply become intolerant of children's behavior in our culture. A related issue is that of the age of a child relative to his or her classmates. If a child is a year younger than some classmates, then we would expect huge differences in maturation and development. And the younger the child, the more pronounced is the developmental lags associated with age differences.

This is a prime example of trying to correct "normal" behavior. It is also a prime example of how poor child placement in the school system can result in a serious, and perhaps, lifelong struggle. Children labelled as needing help think of themselves differently. Self-worth is eroded. They do not do well academically and their career options can be thwarted. Table 4.15 shows the increased probability of a child being labelled as ADHD if they were born in December than if born in January.

Table 4.15   Immaturity of ADHD?

• Canadian Sample: 937,943 children 6–12 years of age
• Born in December: boys 30% (7.4% vs. 5.7%) and girls 70% (2.7% vs. 1.6%) more likely to be diagnosed with ADHD than if born in January
• 5.5% of boys and 1.6% of girls received treatment for ADHD

Source: Morrow et al. (2012).

More parents are becoming mindful of this problem of starting children in school at too young an age. It is a good example of how holding the child back a year may actually result in far superior overall academic performance.

DIET

Researchers Molly E. Waring and Kate L. Lapane from the Brown University Medical School report that ADHD children not currently using medication were 1.5 times more likely to be overweight as compared to non-ADHD children. Children taking medication for ADHD, however, were

1.6 times more likely of being underweight compared to children without ADHD.

A study in the medical journal *Lancet* (2011) reported that nearly two-thirds of ADHD children who followed a restricted food elimination diet had a significant drop in ADHD symptoms and oppositional/defiant behavior. The author, Dr. Lidy Pelsser, further reported that children who went off the diet relapsed. She concludes that some ADHD children should be diagnosed with "food-induced ADHD."

There appears to be clear links between ADHD and diet. At one level, it appears that some foods have an allergic-like negative effect on children's behavior. In addition, there also appears to be a clear link between being overweight and ADHD. For the latter, the one major way to help prevent childhood weight problems is to encourage regular exercise through physical outdoor play. In a previous section, we discussed the problem of IA. One of the direct effects of IA is poor diet and weight problems. Structuring regular physical outdoor play will not only help with diet problems but will also help to control the other major cognitive, mood, and motivational problems associated with IA.

And there is, of course, our old villain, sugar. Dr. Suglia and colleagues report in the *Journal of Pediatrics* (2013) that studies in Norway and the United States show consistent findings of high soft drink consumption leading to increased behavior problems in five-year-old children. Further, high consumption by pregnant mothers is positively related to behavior problems in children at three years of age.

DRUGS

I hope I am preaching to the choir here! Any parent who turns a blind eye to their child using drugs or alcohol is an abuser. Early in this book, we reviewed the brain assessment of a 13-year-old male child who had markers for ADHD. I reviewed the "flags" in the brain wave assessment that alerted me to the possibility that this child was using drugs, particularly cannabis. I challenged the child, as the reader may recall, and the child admitted to routine use of marijuana.

What made me suspicious was a slowing of the Alpha brain wave peak frequency. Peak frequency of the Alpha brain wave is associated with IQ. Although I assume this is unnecessary, parents should be alerted to the fact that cannabis use severely affects the undeveloped brain. It makes the child, and later the adult, stupid.

A study that spanned a 20 year period reported that "adolescents who start using cannabis persistently before the age of 18 years show a marked decline in measures of intelligence in adulthood even if they stop using the drug along the way" (M. Meier, *Proceedings of the National Academy of Sciences*, August 27, 2012). This is consistent with research that has shown that the child's brain is vulnerable and that exposure to drugs is worse when it occurs early in adolescence. However, more recent research indicates that cannabis use can cause brain structure changes even when use started in late twenties. Further, research reported in the *Journal of Neuroscience* (April 2014) by Dr. Hans Breiter and colleagues indicates that even "causal" (get high once/twice a week) use of this drug causes brain abnormalities. Obviously, parents who believe that causal recreational use, or use to "help him relax," to quote a recent parent of a client, is not harmful are simply wrong.

PRESCRIPTION MEDICATIONS

I hope I am still preaching to the choir as I assume I was when discussing the issues of drugs with children. The cardinal rule, as always, is disciplined and monitored use. Proper use of medication for many of the conditions discussed in this book can be effective for controlling symptoms. More appropriately, in my opinion, medications serve the important function of allowing a bridging between a dysfunctional state and a state of self-regulation where the causes of the symptoms are corrected. Gradual titration from the medication as the self-regulatory procedures become effective completes the process. Unfortunately, drug companies would much prefer lifelong medicated symptom suppression/sedation and appeal directly to the public with obscene advertising, urging clients to request specific medications, often for self-diagnosed problems.

As we have mentioned throughout this book, some drugs used with children have scant evidence for efficacy. Others have limited benefit, although advertised otherwise, such as antidepressants that collectively average about 5 percent benefit over placebo. However, many other of these drugs that have limited benefit also have quite substantial risk of serious side effects. So, it is important to do your homework in order to effectively address the causes of the problem and not simply try to sedate the symptoms.

In a study of over 25,000 individuals with at least one diagnosis of ADHD, the effects of medication on criminality were assessed. This work was done in Sweden by Dr. Lichtenstein and colleagues and published in the *New England Journal of Medicine* (2012). Dr. Lichtenstein reported that the estimated probability of conviction of a crime over a four-year treatment period was reduced by 32 percent for men and 41 percent for women. In the male sample, the likelihood of being convicted of a crime during periods when the individual was not being treated increased by 12 percent. Hence, in this population of individuals with ADHD diagnoses who were hospitalized or outpatients at some point, it demonstrates the efficacy of medication for clients with ADHD.

On the other hand, the Substance Abuse and Mental Health Services Administration (SAMHSA) Drug Warning Network in the United States reports that hospital emergency room visits for negative effects of ADHD stimulant medications tripled from 2005 to 2010 to a record 31,244 visits. Some of the documented side effects include psychotic episodes, insomnia, seizures, headache, exacerbation of tics, nervousness, tremor, dizziness, anorexia, nausea, weight loss, growth retardation, and heart palpitation.

It is important to keep in mind that a report endorsed by the American Pediatric Association ranks biofeedback as a highest level evidence-based non-medication treatment for ADHD. Comparative studies have shown neurotherapy to be comparable to medication in short-term effectiveness for many forms of ADHD. Further, the long-term benefit of treating the ADHD at the neurological level with neurotherapy is superior to medication in most cases since the medication does not appear to result in long-term improvement of the condition.

SUMMARY AND CONCLUSIONS

So, it is pretty obvious how we need to proceed as parents. Minimum of 90 minutes per day of outside physical exercise. No TV, cell phones or any other electronic device, except an alarm clock, in the child's bedroom. Balanced diet heavy on raw fruits and vegetables. Neither medications nor drugs. No Internet use when with parents outside of home. Home use of Internet restricted to 30 minutes per day AFTER homework and household chores completed. No cell phones at the dining table or in family social contexts. Fixed bedtime for appropriate amount of sleep depending on child's age. Family eats meals together at dining room table with focus on listening to children. Major support and encouragement for any extracurricular, self-initiated activity such as chess club, music lessons, swimming, socially appropriate volunteer activities, any team sport, dance, art, and the like. Praise is earned. Mothers outrank everyone. Rules are rules and violations have consequences. "Gifted" refers to Monet, Mozart, Einstein, and Mother Teresa.

Of course, we can elaborate on this list. But we all really know what is needed. The problem is we have to live in the real world and do the best we can!

FIVE

Help at Home and in Schools

Those of you who have just read the summary and conclusions to Chapter Four may well be thinking "Get real!" In our present culture, there is no way that we can implement the suggestions included in that last summary. We live in the real world. Even if we impose very strict regulations and limitations on things like Internet use, our children's friends may well be very heavy Internet users. The pressure on our children to be socially acceptable can be overwhelming. The fact that it is difficult does not mean we should not try.

Internet addiction, for example, is an extraordinarily serious problem. This is particularly true for the ADHD child. The child's neurological condition of elevated slow frequency amplitude simply means they are sitting ducks for addiction to this highly stimulating media. Even more serious is the use of this modality with autistic children and those with Asperger's. I do not think it is unreasonable to say that an Internet addicted autistic child is very likely not to respond favorably to any form of therapy because of this addiction. The child must socially interact if he or she is to acquire social empathy, emotional awareness, and social skills.

So, I think it is fair to start off where we left off in the last chapter. Children respond very well to efficient parenting. Quite simply, this means structure, unquestionable social and emotional support, and emotional and physical safety. Children are praised appropriately pursuant to their accomplishments, but the love of the child's parents for the child is completely independent of any achievements. In short, the child feels safe, loved, and provided with organized and structured living conditions.

Enough preaching about parenting. How can we implement the extremely powerful technology of neurotherapy for the benefit of our children? I think it is now obvious to the reader that labels are absolutely meaningless. They do not provide us with any information; they do not indicate how or why or where we go to treat these conditions; and they are very likely to lead to foolish top-down procedures for treating very divergent and, at times, complex conditions.

Simple ADHD is nothing more than elevated amplitude of slow frequency brain waves over much of the cortex of the brain. What this means is that the brain is hypoactive and the child is having difficulty sustaining focus because of daydreaming and distractibility. In extreme cases, it gives rise to the child's need to move. The brain is hypoactive so the child is self-medicating by bouncing off the walls. This is the type of condition that responds to central nervous system stimulants such as methylphenidate. However, all hyperactive children are different. Some are hyperactive because of elevated slow frequency brain wave amplitude; others may be hyperactive because they are frightened. The unique power and clinical benefit of the ClinicalQ is that it identifies fundamental neurological conditions associated with children's inability to perform well in school. Many, if not most, of the problems associated with poor school achievement have nothing at all to do with ADD or ADHD. They have to do with a myriad of other contributing causes such as bad parenting, bullying, emotional trauma, Internet addiction, family strife, poor sleep hygiene, or neurological conditions such as depression, poor stress tolerance, or emotional volatility.

AT HOME

I like to borrow a page from Dr. John Gottman's therapy for dysfunctional relationships. Dr. Gottman is one of the leading experts in family and marital therapy. I combine Gottman's procedure for emotional processing with the aboriginal healing circle practice. In the healing circle, as I understand it, people sit around the campfire with the talking stick. The stick is passed from one person to another and when you are in possession of the talking stick, you have the unchallengeable right to speak. Other members can only express agreement or acknowledgment. That is, they can say "yes" or "I understand." Nothing more!

I add an additional regulation. The person who holds the talking stick is able to share his or her personal emotional state: to talk about how they feel; what it is they aspire to; challenges they face. No one makes suggestions. No one criticizes. No one offers judgment. They only listen and agree.

John Gottman has a similar procedure that he uses in marital and couple counseling. For a set amount of time, perhaps 20 minutes, the couple shares their emotional experiences. There are a number of rules very similar to the healing circle. The first rule is you only speak about your own feelings. You do not discuss other members of the group; you do not offer suggestions; you do not criticize; you do not judge. If you are the speaker you share about yourself; how you feel; what you have been doing; what you are grateful for; your fears and aspirations; your dreams and fantasies. You do not talk about anybody else in the group. If you are the listener, you listen intently and acknowledge that you understand what the other person is saying; again, no judgment, no suggestions, no criticism. The talking stick or other symbolic item or gesture indicates that the other person in the relationship now has the floor.

I find that it is always useful to terminate this daily routine with a statement of gratitude. This is quite simply a statement of one or two things that has occurred during the day about which you are grateful. It can be that you enjoyed the sunrise when you got up in the morning. You enjoyed your morning cup of coffee. You enjoyed your spouse's smile. You enjoyed the sunset. Research has indicated that one should be "grateful for gratitude!" People who are grateful are much better off than those who are not. As one of my clients perceptively stated: "Grateful for the breeze in one's face, not the Mercedes in the garage!"

And, in this context, I encourage clients to acknowledge that simple things can have a profound effect on the emotional climate of the family. We can include our children in this very simple procedure. For couples, I advise that this healing circle exercise be done in private and in a neutral environment (i.e., not the bedroom or the dinner table). For the family, however, when everybody is sitting at the dining table for meals can be a very good venue for this to occur. All family members can take turns to talk about what they have done during the day; what has happened; what worked and what did not; how they are feeling about their dreams and aspirations; what is up for tomorrow; are they happy. The focus moves around the table until everybody has had the chance to share. Then one family member (many find it is beneficial to rotate this among family members) can simply summarize what everyone has said. This healing circle process is concluded with a simple ritual of identifying a few things for which the family is thankful (e.g., Johnny got a B in his math test; Dad had wonderful minestrone soup for lunch; Grandma had a most beautiful day in her garden). People with religious foundations may want to incorporate this within their religious metaphor. But that is not necessary: This can simply be a statement of fact.

It is quite clear that this simple focus on gratitude can have very beneficial effects on the emotional climate of the family.

The reader may recall research reported earlier in this book indicating that the more family dinners per week reported by children victimized by cyber bullying, the less symptomatic the child. It is quite apparent that the payoff for focusing on positive family emotional climate with open and supportive emotional communication cannot be overrated!

NOW TO THE NEUROLOGY

As indicated in earlier chapters, if we are able to do a clinical EEG on any child who is having a problem in school, then we are able to identify very precisely what the nature of the problem is: what areas of the brain are affected, whether there is likely to be trauma involved, and whether the child is experiencing reactive depression. If it is neurological in nature, such as the ADD in which there is elevated slow frequency amplitude, then there are a few things that we can do immediately to assist this child to improve focus. This can include the harmonics that have been found to suppress slow frequency amplitude and can be extremely effective for helping the child do homework more efficiently. Figures 5.1–5.5 show some of the impact of a particular harmonic referred to as OMNI that suppresses slow frequency amplitude and can be used by children who experience difficulty sustaining attention. There are other such products, but this particular product has considerable research behind it. Played softly in the background, it suppresses elevated Theta, elevated slow frequency amplitude, thereby helping the child be more focused and attentive. Many college students use this product, not because they have any particular ADD problems, but it simply helps them to sustain focus more efficiently, rather like the effects of a caffeinated drink.

However, I would like to emphasize that before we take any action, like the use of a medication or harmonic sound, or any other procedure to help the child focus, we should first attend to structure. Does the child have a quiet place to study? Are all electronic instruments, other than an alarm clock, removed from the environment? Is the child's homework structured and scheduled at a fixed time during the day, as early as possible, to mitigate fatigue factors? Is a parent immediately available to help, comfort, support, and encourage the child while doing these tasks? When the tasks are completed, does the child have something to look forward to, such as the undivided attention of the parent?

HARMONICS

Keeping in mind that a structured, interference-free environment for the child to be able to do homework is far more important than any study aid or treatment that you may employ, there are a number of products designed for home use that can help with increased cognitive efficiency. It is important when using any self-help product that one ask a very simple question: Where are the supporting data? And testimonial data are worthless. The following two self-help products are simply auditory subthreshold presentations of binaural beat frequencies that were popular self-help products developed decades ago. If two tones of close frequency and amplitude are combined, what one hears is a beat frequency that is the difference between the frequencies of the tones. For example, if you hear 200 Hz combined with 210 Hz one hears a 10 Hz beat.

Over the past 25 years I have been doing a substantial amount of research into the effects of certain sounds on the neurological activity of the brain. One of the discoveries I have made is that subliminal presentation of certain sounds can markedly affect brain wave activity. Interestingly, the effect of the same sound supraliminally; that is, you can hear it, is substantially different from the effect it has when it is below hearing threshold. For example, if you listen to an audible 10 Hz beat frequency one finds that the body tends to show physiological indicators of relaxation. However, if that same sound is presented below hearing threshold, the body shows the reverse, namely physiological indicators of increased arousal (e.g., increased heat rate). It is interesting to note that other researchers have found that there are differences between the effects of stimulation presented above and below recognition thresholds. Dr. Gary Schwartz at Arizona State University, in his personal communication, found a similar effect in olfaction and Dr. Len Ochs found a similar kind of effect in visual perception.

Two harmonics have been found to be effective for helping children concentrate in school and while doing homework. One, called OMNI (includes a 10 Hz beat frequency), suppresses slow frequency (Theta) amplitude. As discussed earlier, elevated Theta amplitude can cause inattentiveness. When there is a marked elevation of Theta amplitude, hyperactivity can be the problem. OMNI suppresses Theta amplitude so it improves attention and reduces the hyperactivity. The second harmonic, called SERENE (includes a 25 Hz beat frequency), does the reverse. SERENE reduces Beta amplitude and also usually increases Theta amplitude. This quiets the brain and thus helps with children who cannot concentrate due to hyper-arousal and anxiety.

Figure 5.1   Effects of OMNI on suppression of Theta amplitude

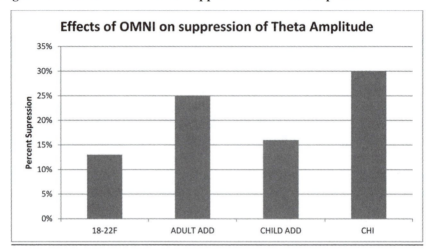

Since OMNI suppresses slow frequency amplitude, it is a good home aid for a child with an ADD problem related to elevated slow frequency amplitude. OMNI works extraordinarily well for helping the child focus. Figure 5.1 shows the efficacy of this harmonic on suppressing slow frequency amplitude for college students, children with ADD, adults with ADD, and those with traumatic brain injury.

It is also interesting to note that there are some gains associated with the use of these harmonics over a period of time. One such study was done by one of my graduate students, Françoise Dupont (Dupont, F., & Swingle, P. G. (1996, August). *Troubles déficitaires de l'attention et réduction de l'activité cérébrale theta par une technique subliminale auditive.* Paper presented at the International Congress of Psychology, Montreal, Quebec.) who found that over an eight-week period, the amplitude of slow frequency brain wave activity decreased by about 10 percent with daily use of OMNI. Figure 5.2 shows the weekly change with a group of children who only used the OMNI harmonic and had no other neurotherapy treatments during the eight-week test period.

The average suppression of slow frequency amplitude when listening to the OMNI harmonic is up to about 30 percent for some groups. However, it can be much greater and, of course, much lower as well. It does not seem to be effective for about 15 percent of people in treatment. In general, if the suppression rate is above 5 percent during the ClinicalQ assessment, it is prescribed for home use. Figure 5.3 shows that Theta suppression is greatest

Figure 5.2   Effects of OMNI home use on cumulative Theta suppression

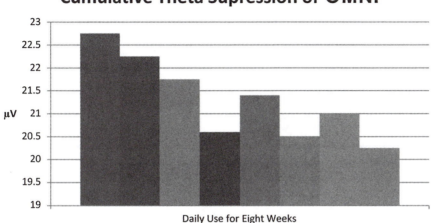

Cumulative Theta Supression of **OMNI**

Daily Use for Eight Weeks

for people over 18 but does not differ significantly between males and females. The range is about 30 percent suppression for the over 18-year-old group and about 17 percent for children under 18 years of age. This Theta suppression is substantial and compares very favorably with any medication that is designed to excite the sensory motor cortex, such as methylphenidate. Children simply listen to this harmonic playing very softly in the background. Because OMNI is played at very low volume, it is not intrusive. It effectively suppresses the excess slow frequency amplitude, thus helping the child to sustain focus for longer periods of time.

As shown in Figure 5.4, it is helpful to look at the full brain wave spectrum to determine the effects of harmonics on all brain wave amplitudes. A brain stimulant can be very helpful for many people in addition to those with ADHD problems. Figure 5.4 shows the effects, on an older male client, of listening to OMNI for two minutes. These data were provided by the late Dr. Thomas Budzynski (personal communication). As the data indicate, OMNI not only suppressed Theta amplitude but also suppressed slow Alpha amplitude. But, most importantly, it increased the amplitude of fast Alpha. This is a very effective treatment for clients complaining of reduced cognitive efficiency, and failing memory, such as can occur in age-related cognitive declines.

If the child's problem is not one of elevated slow frequency amplitude but rather a problem with elevated fast frequency in the back of the brain resulting in poor stress tolerance, racing thoughts, and anxiety, then the

Figure 5.3   Theta suppression as a function of age and gender

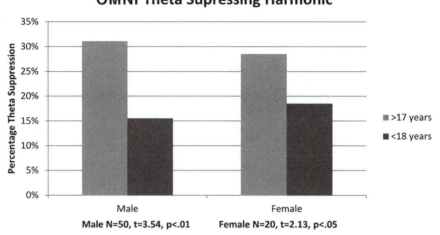

Figure 5.4   Full EEG spectrum effects of OMNI with older male client

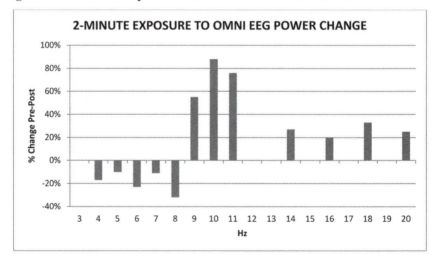

SERENE harmonic is very effective for quieting the child and thereby helping to sustain focus and attention. SERENE suppresses elevated fast frequency in the occipital (back) region of the brain. Figure 5.5 shows the suppressive effect on the fast frequency brain wave amplitudes associated with having this sound playing softly in the background.

Figure 5.5   Suppression of Beta amplitude while listening to SERENE. Cz is the center top of the head; Fz is middle of front of the head; O1 is the back of the head

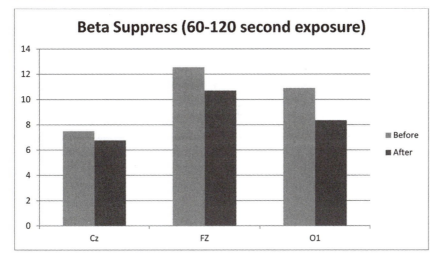

SAFE ROOMS AND IN-SCHOOL NEUROTHERAPY PROGRAMS

A very insightful application of these harmonics in the school system was proposed by Dr. Mary Jo Sabo, a psychologist consulting for the Yonkers School Board. Dr. Sabo developed what she called "Safe Rooms." Children who have become disruptive, inattentive, or emotionally dysregulated in the classroom can go to the Safe Room and listen to one of the harmonics to help themselves gain control and self-regulate. Once they feel as though they are able to self-regulate, they can return to the classroom. This makes so much more sense than punishing the child by putting them out in the hallway, or sending them to the principal's office, or the many other punishing and stigmatizing things we do when children become disruptive. Safe Rooms help the child learn how to self-regulate. Adding the neurologically active harmonics helps the child gain control more rapidly.

There are a number of schools around the country that have tried the Safe Room concept. Some preliminary data from a number of these schools indicate that the amount of time spent in the Safe Room decreases, in some cases by about a third, and the number of visits to the Safe Room decrease over time, as the child learns to self-regulate. For example, a Safe Room with the SERENE harmonic was introduced in a school for troubled children. Preliminary data indicate that time in the Safe Room decreased from about

11 minutes to about 8 minutes and the frequency of visits to the room reduced by 10 percent. These data were collected over a few weeks following introduction of the Safe Room procedures.

These are all very promising data associated with the use of this technology to assist the child with self-regulation. We are applying a similar procedure in our outreach programs for homeless populations in Vancouver. In this context, we have safe areas where a person can sit and listen to one of the harmonics, which helps them to reduce mental stress, gain control, and self-regulate. However, a major benefit of neurotherapy would be to offer ClinicalQ assessments as a Resource Room activity in schools. Children who are having difficulty in class would be offered the opportunity to have a ClinicalQ assessment completed by the Resource Room teacher. This very rapid six minute recording-time procedure could realistically save not only thousands of dollars for the school but, more importantly, literally save the lives of troubled/challenged children. All we have to do is look at Table 2.1 in Chapter Two that shows the statistics of the relationship of untreated ADHD in the adult population to criminality and irresponsible sexual conduct. Our prisons are loaded with individuals who have very treatable ADHD conditions. Had they been identified at an early age and treated appropriately, not just sedated, society would have benefited enormously, the school systems would have saved tens of thousands of dollars, and many lives would be saved.

I assume it comes as no surprise to readers that many schools are very resistant to implementation of this technology. In the case of the Swingle Clinic, we have offered this service for free to a number of schools and have been turned down flat. We have had similar experiences with agencies that provide services to the homeless. When agencies or services become parasitic on the problem, any potential change to the status quo is resisted. However, the politics of this obscenity is beyond the scope of this book.

There are several pilot projects around the country, for which we have been consulting, where neurotherapy has been introduced into the school program. Our findings are very straightforward. First of all, we do not just routinely test and assess every child. There is no need to do that. Children who are experiencing difficulties, who would normally be referred to the resource room teacher, are offered a very simple assessment to identify the areas of the brain that are associated with the difficulty. Again, the power of the ClinicalQ is that it may identify other areas that are problematic. And in this circumstance, the school counselors would become involved to determine if this child is safe. However, if it is ADHD, it can be readily improved with basic neurotherapeutic treatments that can be administered as a resource room activity.

SIX

Neurotherapeutic Treatment: For Conditions Affecting the Child's Ability to Learn

In the present chapter, we will review in detail the neurotherapeutic treatment procedures used to correct the neurological conditions adversely affecting the child's ability to learn efficiently in school. As has been pointed out in numerous areas throughout this book, we want to work from the bottom-up, not the top-down. It is perfectly obvious, as some of the case studies have illustrated, that a child's ability to focus and learn can be affected by many variables. The power of working from the bottom-up is that the brain assessment will precisely identify why the child is having a problem with learning. It will also precisely identify the areas of the brain that require attention to correct those problems.

Many mistakes are made with top-down procedures. Top-down provides labels for clusters of symptoms but does not give any information about what areas of the brain need treatment to correct those symptoms. Top-down tries to identify fixed, one-size-fits-all treatments for symptom clusters. However, as we have seen, identical symptoms can have many causes including brain function inefficiencies, brain injury, behavioral problems, emotional problems, family problems, and Internet addiction, to name a few. The treatment based on symptoms approach then turns out to be a trial and error approach which is clearly inefficient relative to following the neurology. The top-down problem certainly relates to medication and it is equally problematic to the area of neurotherapy.

We have ample examples of children being medicated because of problematic family conditions, incompetent parenting, or the child being frightened or insecure or unhappy. In short, we want to be sure that we are treating the right condition. The most efficient way of determining that we are treating the correct condition is to do a diagnostic EEG that will point out, very precisely, areas of the brain that are not functioning efficiently. Once these areas are identified, and we verify that the child is experiencing learning problems consistent with these neurological anomalies, we can then proceed to normalize brain functioning.

I start this chapter with data from studies on identical twins. Table 6.1 shows data from twin studies designed to identify genetic predisposition to schizophrenia. As you will note, if one monozygotic twin has schizophrenia, the probability that the second twin will also have schizophrenia is as high as 50 percent. The interesting statistic is that 50 percent will not! We also see the heritability factor for dizygotic twins and biological siblings in which the heritability factor is approximately 15 percent. Again, 85 percent will not show symptoms associated with schizophrenia even though their dizygotic twin, or sibling, suffers from schizophrenia.

Table 6.1   Heritability Statistics on Schizophrenia

Genetic Predispositions

Monozygotic Twins	30–50%
Dizygotic Twins	15%
Siblings	15%
General Population	1%

Adopted-Biological Relatives with Schizophrenia

Adoptee with Schizophrenia	13%
Adoptee without Schizophrenia	2%

Source: Gottesman (1991).

These data are important for several reasons. First, it points out that "genetic" does not mean "in concrete." Heritability means that a person has a predisposition to a certain condition but something is required to trigger the manifestation of that predisposition. These data also speak to brain plasticity in the sense that genetic predisposition does not mean inevitable outcome. The data on adopted children show similar patterns. If an adopted child has a biological relative with schizophrenia, the probability that that child will develop schizophrenia is about 13 percent. For adopted children without schizophrenic biological relatives, the probability of schizophrenia manifesting is about 2 percent, indicating that the heritability factor is about 11 percent.

These data are important for another reason. They point out why it is essential to use a clinical database as opposed to a normative database. The ClinicalQ, as the name implies, uses data from clinical clients to identify areas of problematic brain functioning. Using the case of schizophrenia, for example, the monozygotic twin who has schizophrenia would be placed in the clinical database. The second monozygotic twin with exactly the same genetic load, but without manifested schizophrenia, would be a candidate for the normative database. The result is that a normative database is likely to be statistically blind to predisposition to this condition.

Similar data show similar problems with clients with predisposition to depressed mood states. Those with manifested depression are in the clinical database whereas those with the same predisposition that has not manifested are candidates for the normative database. Hence again, the normative database is likely to be statistically blind to many forms of neurological predisposition to depression.

NEUROTHERAPY

There are three general classes of treatment associated with neurotherapy. The first is brain wave biofeedback or neurofeedback. This is the form of neurotherapeutic treatment that most people are familiar with. Brain wave biofeedback is based on the concept of instrumental conditioning. When the brain is doing what we want it to do, the client hears a sound or sees something move on the computer monitor. For children, we can set it up so the child is playing a video game with her or his brain. When the brain is doing what we want it to do, the child hears a tone and icons move on the computer screen. The game can be something like Pac-Man, rocket ships passing through mazes, or airplanes flying though targets.

The second class of treatments is *brain driving*. Brain driving incorporates concepts of classical conditioning. These procedures involve exposing the client to stimulation such as lights, sounds, electromagnetic stimulation, or electrical stimulation of acupuncture points to nudge the brain to move in the desired direction. So, for example, if we wanted to reduce the strength of slow frequency amplitude in the brain, every time the amplitude of the slow frequency crosses a specified training threshold, lights might come on that suppress slow frequency amplitude. We know the lights will have this neurological property of suppressing slow frequency amplitude because we pretest all of the stimuli that are used to determine that they do, in fact, affect the brain in the desired manner.

The third class of treatments are home-based. We may ask the client to listen to certain sounds in the home environment to stimulate the brain. Such stimulant sounds can be used by children to help them do homework more efficiently or by the elderly to brighten up their brain while reading. Sounds that quiet the brain are used at home for relaxation and to improve sleep quality. The use of harmonics at home (and school) as part of the neurotherapy treatment regimen is described in Chapter Five.

NEUROFEEDBACK

As Figure 6.1 shows, the setup for brain wave biofeedback, also called neurofeedback, with a child involves placing electrodes on each earlobe (other areas of the body can be used for grounding and reference such as the mastoid prominence behind the ears) and an active electrode on top of the head. For common ADD (CADD), we typically place the electrode at the center of the head as shown in this figure. From that location, all of the brain wave amplitudes are being monitored, but for treatment of CADD we are reducing the strength or amplitude of Theta (3–7 Hz).

Figure 6.1   Set-up for brain wave biofeedback

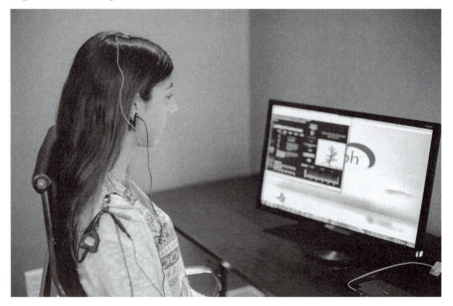

Figure 6.2 shows one of the games that we typically use with children. It is a simulation of an airplane flying through target areas. The airplane movement is dependent on the child's brain activity. For the treatment of CADD, with the electrode on top center of the head, the airplane would move toward the target area when the amplitude of Theta decreases. For example, the child whose brain wave topograph is shown in Figure 6.3 had a Theta amplitude of 17 microvolts (*mv*) when she started. I set the training threshold so that when Theta amplitude dropped below 16*mv*, the airplane accelerated. When the Theta amplitude went above 16*mv* the airplane stopped. This is an instrumental conditioning procedure. Responses we want to facilitate (reduced amplitude of Theta) are rewarded with movement of the airplane. Events that we do not want to encourage (no change or an increase in Theta amplitude) are not rewarded—the airplane stops.

Figure 6.2   Airplane game used for neurofeedback. (Zukor's Air feedback game by Zukor Interactive. Used by permission.)

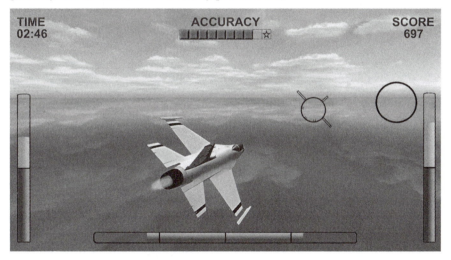

There are a number of important parameters associated with neurofeedback training. The movements of the icon (e.g., airplane) that is the reward must occur in close proximity to the brain wave amplitude change. That is, the contingency must be close so that the brain learns that reduced Theta strength is associated with reward. There are many other learning theory parameters that are important for efficient training (learning) of brain wave activity, but the reward/response contingency is one of the most important.

Figure 6.3   Brain wave topograph showing elevated slow frequency amplitude

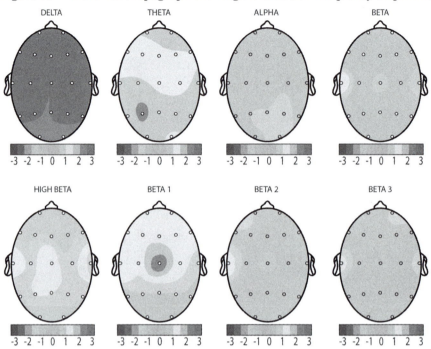

As the child gets better at reducing Theta amplitude, we lower the training threshold. For example, when the child starts to learn to decrease the amplitude of Theta we might set the difficulty level so that the airplane moves about 70 percent of the time. When her success moves up to 80 or 90 percent, then we raise the difficulty level so that it goes back down to 70 percent. In this way, we are always moving toward lower and lower Theta amplitudes. The training procedure is very similar to that used by high jumpers. As they get better at clearing the bar, the bar is raised.

At the clinic, we are very cautious about our selection of neurofeedback games that the child plays. The game should be moderately interesting to sustain the child's interest and attention. We do not want a highly exciting game because then the child's interest will be sustained by high levels of arousal. A critical mistake often made by inexperienced neurotherapists is changing the training game because the child claims to be bored with the present game. Children with attention problems are going to complain that the games are boring. After they have played the game for a while, their attention wanes, just as it does in school. The now bored child will then frequently ask for a new game. The inexperienced neurotherapist will often respond to this request with a change in the training game. When this happens, the neurotherapist has become part of the problem. The child's attention is being maintained by a change in the stimulating properties of the task (i.e., new game). So if the neurotherapist falls into this trap, the child is going to require many more sessions. Worse, in some circumstances, the child's condition will not improve sufficiently because the neurology is not changing due to the child's focus is being maintained by stimulation changes.

BRAIN DRIVING

Brain driving incorporates the principles of classical conditioning. The reader may recall the seminal work of Ivan Pavlov who demonstrated that the salivation response of a dog could be conditioned to the sound of a bell. The way Pavlov did this was to put a small amount of meat powder on the dog's tongue (an unconditioned stimulus for salivation) while he simultaneously rang a bell. After a number of pairings of the meat powder with the bell, Pavlov just rang the bell and was able to show that the bell elicited the salivation response. Herbert Jasper and Charles Shagass, in the 1940s at McGill University, demonstrated that brain wave amplitude could be conditioned in exactly the same way as Pavlov did with his dogs.

We use similar principles in brain driving: we use stimuli that we know have a high probability of affecting the brain in a very specific manner. There are sounds we have developed that we know have a high probability of suppressing low frequency amplitude (Theta). We have other sounds that we know will increase specific wave forms. And we have known for some time that flashing lights will suppress some brain wave amplitudes. Decades ago, Drs. Adrian and Mathews (*Brain*, 1934) also reported that flashing lights can entrain brain wave amplitude. For example, if a light at 11 cycles per second is flashed into the eye, there will be an increase in amplitude of the 11 Hz brain wave.

For brain driving, we combine a number of different stimuli that have the properties of either suppressing or enhancing particular wave forms. We make this contingent on brain activity. For example, if the brain is starting to put out too much slow frequency amplitude, we stimulate with light (e.g., at 16 Hz) or a sound that will suppress the slow frequency amplitude. Conversely, if we find that the amplitude of the desired brain wave is dropping, then we might apply a sound that has the property of increasing the amplitude of that particular brain wave.

Brain wave brain driving can be used to nudge the brain into more desirable ranges. One of the most powerful applications is in the context of tasking. *Tasking* simply means that we ask the child to read and summarize, or read and write a sentence or two, about the paragraph that was just read, or do mathematical problems, or work on puzzles, or organize objects according to shape, or any other task that may be relevant to the child's academic inefficiencies.

Figure 6.4 shows the glasses that are worn by the child while doing tasking. There are lights around the periphery of the lens so that the lights can go on or off depending on brain wave amplitudes, as just described. The child can look right through the clear lenses, so the child can be reading or writing or doing math problems while the brain is being stimulated. For adults, as shown in Figure 6.5, acupuncture points can be electrically stimulated; other stimuli that we know have specific effects on brain wave functioning can also be presented.

Figure 6.4   Goggles for light stimulation used during brain driving tasking

Figure 6.5   Brain driving preparation showing stimulation with lights and sound plus electrical stimulation of acupuncture points

Figures 6.6 and 6.7 show the written output of a child who had been diagnosed as having Written Output Disorder (WOD). Our thinking about WOD has changed much like our thinking about sleep disorders has changed. We now think of sleep problems as the cause, rather than as a symptom, of some other disorder, as we had in the past. For example, we now consider the sleep problem as the potential cause or exacerbator of depression, rather than as a symptom of depression.

With WOD, it is the reverse. We now consider written output problems to be more of a symptom of some other disorder rather than a disorder in itself. Children have written output problems for a number of reasons, and the power of brain driving is that the area of the brain that is inefficient can be under direct treatment while the child is engaged in writing. So, we are treating the cause of the output problem and monitoring the symptom rather than trying to improve output by attempting to remediate the symptom with repetitive drills. As shown in Figures 6.6 and 6.7, there was a marked change in this child's ability to write and communicate in written form. It is important to note that the change shown here took place over just three sessions. Brain driving is that powerful!

Figure 6.6   First writing sample of child diagnosed with WOD

Figure 6.7   Written output of child during third brain driving session

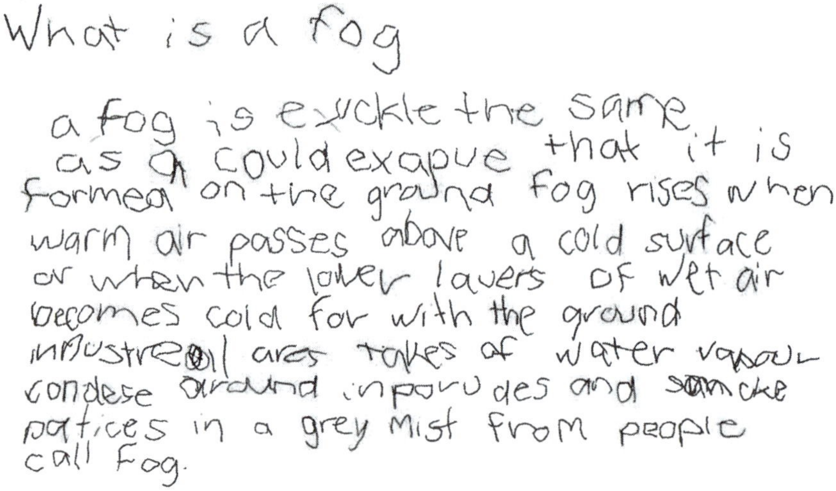

What is a fog

a fog is ewckle the same
as a could exapue that it is
formed on the ground fog rises when
warm air passes above a cold surface
or when the lower layers of wet air
becomes cold for with the ground
industreal aras tokes of water vapour
condese around inporu des and somcke
patices in a grey mist from people
call fog.

CONCLUSIONS

As I have been repeating throughout this book, treatment directed at symptoms and those directed at diagnostic labels have much poorer efficacy results as compared with those directed at the underlying neurological condition. This is true of both neurotherapy as well as with medications. One-size-fits-all protocols for ADHD are of limited efficacy. In the field of neurotherapy, the Theta/Beta protocol in which the amplitude of Theta is reduced and the amplitude of Beta is increased, primarily over the central area of the brain, helps many children with ADHD, but the extent of the improvement and the number of children who do not respond is markedly higher than neurologically targeted procedures.

Likewise with medications. Methylphenidate (e.g., Ritalin) works well with the same population of children that respond well to the Theta/Beta neurotherapy protocol. But this medication does not work well, and in fact may exacerbate other neurological forms of ADHD, such as that associated with elevated frontal Alpha amplitude.

We have known for some time now (from the research of Dr. Vince Monastra and his colleagues, published in 2002 in the *Journal of Applied Psychophysiology and Biofeedback*) that children of parents who use consistent reinforcing parenting strategies have much better neurofeedback outcomes. So, as emphasized throughout this book, competent and empathic parenting really counts! Everything works better with good parenting.

Most important to remember, however, is that the labels just do not matter. The treatment strategy that gives the best outcomes is bottom-up. What does the neurology tell us? If there are no neurological anomalies that are logical bases for the child's reported learning and/or behavioral problems, then we need to investigate more thoroughly to determine the actual causes of the child's cognitive and emotional difficulties. Further, the brain wave assessments will also frequently alert us to other contributing factors to the child's problems.

Conclusions

Children have difficulty in school for many reasons, and the cause of these difficulties can vary markedly. Children may not be able to pay attention because they are frightened, because they are depressed, because they have poor stress tolerance, because they live in unsafe environments, because of family strife and dysfunction, and because their parents are not capable of adequate parenting for any one of a number of reasons.

ADHD is a real condition. There are several forms of neurological dysregulation that are associated with the various forms of ADHD; however, there are many other conditions that mimic ADHD with symptoms that are the same, or similar.

The problem with top-down diagnostic procedures, in which we look at the symptoms associated with the child's academic difficulties, is that the label does not provide us with any information about how to go about treating the condition. And the presumption is that we should be able to medicate the child to facilitate attention and to decrease hyperactivity.

The data are clear that medications for attention do improve performance and help the child to be more attentive. But, the medication must be specific to the form of ADHD as identified by the QEEG. Methylphenidate works for CADD, in which there is a marked elevation of slow frequency (Theta) amplitude over the sensory motor cortex, yet it does not work and, in fact, worsens the high frontal Alpha amplitude form of ADHD. Furthermore, the data are quite clear in showing that medication does not result in any sustained academic or behavioral benefits. The effects of medications for ADHD fade over time as the child develops tolerance to the drugs.

And, children's symptoms do get worse when they are taken off these medications because the child's physiology has adapted to the drug. This worsening has the result of leading parents to believe in the efficacy of the medications when, in fact, it is similar to effects adults experience when giving up smoking.

There is a role for medicating ADHD children. And it is a very important role. When we are dealing with severe conditions such as out-of-control hyperactivity, judicial and prudent use of these medications can help stabilize the child to make the child available for other therapies; most importantly, for neurotherapy. As the brain improves, the medication is systematically titrated out of the treatment regimen. When those who are medicating the child collaborate with neurotherapists, miracles happen for these severely dysfunctional children.

But the broader issue here is that proper assessment of the dysfunctional child's condition will result in everyone involved treating the correct condition. This does not mean focusing on checklists and other evaluative procedures, for categorizing symptoms and forming nosologies that, in turn, dictate treatments for trial and error evaluation. It means obtaining an EEG that is compared with a clinical, *not* a normative, database. The issue is how a particular child's EEG compares with other children with the same symptoms.

And one learns as much when one observes no match for ADHD patterns! The lack of match directs the therapist to assess other EEG patterns indicative of other conditions affecting the child's learning and social behavior. In short, the child's ADHD is a symptom (correlated effect) of some other condition. Treat the base condition and the ADHD symptoms are corrected. It is that straightforward. Treat the underlying condition, not the symptom. This, of course, has been the thrust of this book. Symptom checklist leading to label leading to treatment protocol is simply not efficient. There are many conditions, as we have seen, that do not match the ADHD neurological patterns, but these conditions are associated with symptoms that mimic those of ADHD. And we know that neurotherapy is a very effective evidence-based treatment for the many other non-ADHD conditions that affect children's well-being in school, at home, and in society. Thus, as I have urged throughout this book, treat the condition, not the label.

APPENDIX

Finding a QUALIFIED Neurotherapist

There is an old saying among psychotherapists that clients have difficulty in finding a good match because only about 15 percent of therapists are competent, and of that limited number, the client will get along with only about 15 percent. This wry observation is overdrawn, of course, but the point is that not all therapists, or therapeutic approaches, are right for you. This is also true of neurotherapists. Further, brain wave therapy is not a stand-alone therapy but must be integrated with other therapies. In selecting a neurotherapist, you should insist upon several basic requirements. These include: an independent license to practice in a bona fide health care field within the practitioner's jurisdiction; certified training in neurotherapy; and considerable relevant experience. If possible, you should also be referred by a former client of the therapist.

Let us take a look at these requirements in order. First, the neurotherapist must hold an independent license within the jurisdiction of the therapist's practice. Thus, the person should hold a license to practice psychology, medicine, or some other relevant health care profession. For example, the person doing neurotherapy might be a neurologist, psychologist, psychiatrist, naturopathic physician, licensed clinical social worker, chiropractor, registered clinical counselor, or a medical doctor. The discipline should be relevant to the disorder that you wish to have treated. For example, a chiropractor would probably not be as suitable as a psychologist for a traumatic stress problem, even though both are experienced neurotherapists. Be sure that the person is licensed, certified, or registered by the governmental jurisdiction where the person practices and not simply certified by some professional organization or non-jurisdictional government. A practitioner who does not hold a jurisdictional (e.g., state or province) license to practice a health care profession may claim to be "nationally certified." This national certification can be a meaningless certification related to a mail-order course. There are several reasons to select a neurotherapist who is an independently licensed health care professional. First, he or she has something to lose if the treatment is incompetent or unethical. Professional licensing and registration boards or colleges maintain review boards to field client complaints. These professional practice review boards can censure, suspend, or revoke licenses to practice or can impose strict requirements and conditions to limit the practice of violators. Unlicensed practitioners have no such government-mandated monitoring agency to which they are responsible. They can be psychological or medical hobbyists whose commitment to your treatment is not grounded in systematic training, proper supervision, and accountability to an agency of authority. The second reason to select licensed practitioners is that they carry professional liability insurance. A psychological, or medical, hobbyist may carry business insurance, but professional liability (malpractice) insurance is what matters for the client.

The practitioner should have relevant therapeutic training to treat the disorder for which you seek help. When you consult with a health care provider, you seek a remedy for a disorder and not necessarily a specific treatment method. If you suffer from migraine headaches, for example, relief from the headaches is the central goal of any therapy. You may wish to pursue biofeedback, but the biofeedback should be administered by a practitioner with other treatment options. Thus, a medical physician may be able to use biofeedback in your treatment, but that is not the only treatment option. Similarly a psychologist may offer neurotherapy as a treatment possibility, but she or he has other options such as biofeedback, relaxation therapies, and other psychotherapies to treat the same disorder.

The agency that certifies neurotherapy training is the Biofeedback Certification International Alliance (BCIA). You should select individuals certified in neurofeedback (EEG biofeedback). These certified individuals have training and experience at a specific, albeit minimal, level. I would only select a neurotherapist who has been certified by this agency because it demonstrates that the therapist has submitted her or his credentials for scrutiny and that the board has accepted those credentials as satisfying a specific standard of training and experience.

Because of the growing problem of minimally qualified medical/ psychological hobbyists purporting to practice neurotherapy, be cautious of the growing number of organizations who support one-size-fits-all franchise-like operations in which unlicensed, uncertified, and minimally trained individuals use fixed treatments for everything. These operations do vary in sophistication. Some use only one treatment for every condition, claiming that if brain functioning is temporarily disturbed in treatment, the brain will reorganize toward more normative functioning. Other franchises offer several treatment options which the franchisee selects based on the client's self-report. Thus, if the client claims to suffer from depression, the franchisee might administer a treatment over the front of the head designed to decrease the amplitude of Alpha brain waves. This does work for one form of depression but is ineffective for other forms of depression; or worse, can exacerbate the condition. There are many forms of depression and one-size-fits-all treatment of these conditions is irresponsible.

A related concern with the one-size-fits-all treatment and unqualified neurotherapy practitioners is that they do not have the essential expertise to deal with the total condition of the client. Clients who come for treatment require more than simply realigning the brain wave functioning. They often require psychological and/or behavioral therapy as well. An example of this problem is a depressed client who has been exposed to a severe emotional stressor at some point in their life. This client is likely to have a major emotional abreaction during treatment of depression. Practitioners unqualified to deal with these situations can cause significant psychological damage to such clients.

The last factor to consider in the selection of a neurotherapist is the level of experience they have with cases similar to yours. It takes five days to train a person to do a few basic neurotherapy protocols. It takes several thousand supervised treatment sessions before one can be considered an expert. Inexperienced therapists tend to rely only on research they read rather than what they have witnessed and accomplished in their own practice. For example, when a child has attention problems, four out of five of them will experience a 50 percent improvement with 40 to 80 sessions of Theta suppress/Beta enhance EEG feedback at the top of the head. When the treatment is done by an expert, a person experienced with hundreds of cases, these treatment statistics can be remarkably different. With CADD, for example, experienced neurotherapists with fully equipped offices and skills in behavior therapy can claim success rates of over 90 percent and with markedly fewer sessions.

Some therapists are more effective than other therapists with equivalent or more years of experience. Every discipline has gifted practitioners, be it music, art, medicine, architecture, psychology, or neurotherapy. Examining the practitioner's credentials will provide the client with only a basic understanding of how well trained and experienced the practitioner is. The only way to find the truly talented neurotherapist is asking former clients of the practitioner. The gifted therapists gain deserved reputations for helping their patients. However, when relying on the recommendation of former clients, keep in mind that a therapist skilled in the treatment of, say, depression may be inexperienced in the treatment of traumatic stress. Hence, even though one hears raving praise of a therapist's treatment, make sure he or she knows how to deal with your problem.

Occasionally, potential clients will ask to speak with clients who have been treated by the practitioner. They believe that by speaking with a former patient they will obtain a valid indication of the therapist's merit. There are several problems with this method. First, therapists are going to refer you to the successes, not the failures. Speaking with a successfully treated client may be reassuring, but it does not provide a valid substitute for important qualifications. Second, I do not put potential clients in touch with my clients because I know very little about the potential client. That person could be problematic and disruptive to my present or former client.

The reverse situation is also a problem. I am frequently asked to recommend therapists in other cities. I often know therapists with excellent professional reputations, but I really know little about their therapeutic effectiveness. I recommend with the disclaimer that I cannot vouch for them as therapists and that the client must make their own assessment after a few visits. All I can tell the person is that the therapist has the necessary training and credentials and that he or she is recognized in the profession.

Clients can often obtain the same information by researching the therapist on the Internet. The therapist's licensing and certifications, if any, are all accessible to the public. Again, finding the truly talented professionals usually happens by word of mouth from previously treated clients.

References

ADHD Parents Medication Guide. (2013). American Academy of Child and Adolescent Psychiatry and American Psychiatric Association. Retrieved from http://www.parentsmedguide.org

Adrian, E. D., & Matthews, B. H. (1934). The Berger rhythm: Potential changes from the occipital lobes in man. *Brain: A Journal of Neurology, 57*, 355–385. doi:10.1093/brain/awp324

Arns, M., Feddema, I., & Kenemansm, J. L. (2014). Differential effects of beta/theta and SMR neurofeedback in ADHD on sleep onset latency. *Frontiers in Human Neuroscience, 8*(1019). doi:10.3389/fnhum.2014.01019

Arseneault, L., Milne, B. J., Taylor, A., Adams, F., Delgado, K., Caspi, A., & Moffitt, T. E. (2008). Being bullied as an environmentally mediated contributing factor to children's internalizing problems: A study of twins discordant for victimization. *Archives of Pediatrics & Adolescent Medicine, 162*(2), 145–150. doi:10.1001/archpediatrics.2007.53

Bambico, F. R., Lacoste, B., Hattan, P. R., & Gobbi, G. (2013). Father absence in the monogamous father mouse impairs social behaviour and modifies dopamine and glutamate synapses in the medial prefrontal cortex. *Cerebral Cortex, 25*(5), 1163–1175. doi:10.1093/cercor/bht310

Barwick, F., Arnett, P., & Slobounov, S. (2012). EEG correlates of fatigue during administration of neuropsychological test battery. *Clinical Neurophysiology, 123*(2), 278–284. doi:10.1016/j.clinph.2011.06.027

Bogart, L. M., Elliott, M. N., Klein, D. J., Tortolero, S. R., Mrug, S., Peskin, M. F., . . . Schuster, M. A. (2014). Peer victimization in fifth grade and health in tenth grade. *Pediatrics, 133*(3), 440–447. doi:10.1542 /peds.2013-3510

Bonuck, K., Rao, T., & Xu, L. (2012). Pediatric sleep disorders and special education need at 8 years: A population-based cohort study. *Pediatrics, 130*(4), 634–642. doi:10.1542/peds.2012-0392

Botash, A. (1997). Examination for sexual abuse in pubertal children: An update. *Pediatric Annals, 26*(5), 312–320.

Bronson, P., & Merryman, A. (2011). *NurtureShock: New thinking about children.* New York, NY: Twelve.

Budzynski, T. H., Budzynski, H. K., Evans, J. R., & Abarbanel, A. (2008). *Introduction to quantitative EEG and neurofeedback: Advanced theory and applications* (2nd ed.). San Diego, CA: Academic.

Chang, A., Aeschbach, D., Duffy, J. F., & Czeisler, C. A. (2014). Evening use of light-emitting eReaders negatively affects sleep, circadian timing, and next-morning alertness. *Proceedings of the National Academy of Sciences, 112*(4), 1232–1237. doi:10.1073/pnas.1418490112

Chiu, S., Nutter, D. A., Palmes, G. K., Pataki, C., Johnson, C., Tegene, B., & Windle, M. L. (2012). *Pediatric Sleep Disorders, 5,* 14–17.

Chrisman, S., & Richardson, L. P. (2014). Prevalence of diagnosed depression in adolescents with history of concussion. *Journal of Adolescent Health, 54*(5), 582–586. doi:10.1016/j.jadohealth.2013.10.006

Copeland, W. E., Wolke, D., Angold, A., & Costello, J. (2013). Adult psychiatric outcomes of bullying and being bullied by peers in childhood and adolescence. *Journal of the American Medical Association, 70*(4), 419–426. doi:10.1001/jamapsychiatry.2013.504

Davidson, R. J. (1992). Anterior cerebral asymmetry and the nature of emotion. *Brain and Cognition, 20*(1), 125–151. doi:10.1016/0278-26 26(92)90065-T

Dupont, F., & Swingle, P. G. (1996, August). *Troubles deficitaires de l'attention et reduction de l'activité cérébrale theta par une technique subliminale auditive.* Paper presented at the International Congress of Psychology, Montreal, Quebec.

Elgar, F. J., Napoletano, A., Saul, G., Dirks, M. A., Craig, W., Poteat, P., . . . Koenig, B. W. (2014). Cyberbullying victimization and mental health in adolescents and the moderating role of family dinners. *Pediatrics, 168*(11), 1015–1022. doi:10.1001/jamapediatrics.2014.1223

Faraone, S. V., & Kunwar, A. R. ADHD in children with comorbid conditions: Diagnosis, misdiagnosis, and keeping tabs on both. *Medscape Psychiatry.* Retrieved from http://www.medscape.org/ psychiatry

Farrar, R., Call, M., & Maples, W. C. (2001). A comparison of the visual symptoms between ADD/ADHD and normal children. *Optometry, 72*(7), 441–451.

Fletcher, J., & Wolfe, B. (2009). Long-term consequences of childhood ADHD on criminal activities. *Journal of Mental Health Policy and Economics, 12*(3), 119–138.

Gilman, J. M., Kuster, J. K., Lee, S., Lee, M. J., Kim, B. W., Makris, N., . . . Breiter, H. C. (2014). Cannabis use is quantitatively associated with nucleus accumbens and amygdale abnormalities in young adult recreational users. *Journal of Neuroscience, 34*(16), 5529–5538. doi:10 .1523/JNEUROSCI.4745-13.2014

Ginsberg, Y., Hirvikoski, T., Grann, M., & Lindefors, N. (2012). Long-term functional outcome in adult prison inmates with ADHD receiving OROS-methylphenidate. *European Archives of Psychiatry and Clinical Neuroscience, 262*(8), 705–724. doi:10.1007/s00406-012-0317-8

Gluck, G. (2011). QEEG accepted in death penalty trial in Florida vs Nelson. *Biofeedback, 39*(2), 74–77. doi: http://dx.doi.org/10.5298/1081 -5937-39.2.04

Gottesman, I. I. (1991). *Schizophrenia Genesis: The origin of madness.* New York: Freeman.

Hagen, H., Moore, K., Wickham, G., & Maples, W. C. (2008). Effect on the EYEPORT system of visual functioning in ADHD children: A pilot study. *Journal of Behavioral Optometry, 19*(2), 37–41.

Hajek, C. A., Yeates, K. O., Taylor, H. G, Bangert, B., Dietrich, A., Nuss, K. E., . . . Wright, M. (2010). Agreement between parents and children on ratings of postconcussive symptoms following mild traumatic brain injury. *Child Neuropsychology, 17*(1), 17–33. doi:10.1080/092 97049.2010.495058

Hamrin, V., & DeSanto, J. (2010). Psychopharmacology of pediatric bipolar disorder. *Expert Review of Neurotherapeutics, 10*(7), 1053–1088. Retrieved from http://www.medscape.com/viewarticle/724852

Hoftun, G. B., Romundstad, P. R., & Rygg, M. (2013). Association of parental chronic pain in the adolescent and young adult. *Archives of Pediatric and Adolescent Medicine, 167*(1), 61–69. doi:10.1001/jamapedi atrics.2013.422

Hudziak, J. J., Albough, M. D., Ducharme, S., Harama, S., Spottswood, M., Evans, A. C., & Botteron, K. N. (2014). Cortical thickness maturation and duration of music training: Health-promoting activities shape brain development. *Journal of American Academy of Child and Adolescent Psychiatry, 53*(11), 1153–1161. doi:10.1016/j.jaac.2014.06.015

Huffman, K. (2013, December 3). Prenatal exposure to alcohol disrupts brain circuitry: No safe level of drinking during pregnancy, neuroscientist says. *Science Daily.* Retrieved from http://sciencedaily.com/releases/2013/12/131203105940.htm

Kaplan, A. (2012, May 8). Anxiety disorders and ADHD: Comorbidity the rule, not the exception. *Psychiatric Times.* Retrieved from http://www.psychiatrictimes.com/apa2012/anxiety-disorders-and-adhd -comorbidity-rule-not-exception#sthash.ILdaT90D.dpuf

Kelly, Y., Kelly, J., & Sacker, A. (2013). Changes in bedtime schedules and behavioral difficulties in 7 year old children. *Pediatrics, 132*(5), 1184–1193. doi:10.1542/peds.2013-1906

Lewis, D. O., Lovely, R., Yaeger, C., Ferguson, G., Friedman, M., Sloane, G., Friedman, H., & Pincus, J. H. (1988). Intrinsic and environmental characteristics of juvenile murderers. *Journal of the American Academy of Child & Adolescent Psychiatry, 27*(5), 582–587. doi:10.1097/00004583-198809000-00011

Lewis, D. O., Pincus, J. H., Bard, B., Richardson, E., Prichep, L. S., Feldman, M., & Yeager, C. (1988). Neuropsychiatric, psycho-educational, and family characteristics of 14 juveniles condemned to death in the United States. *American Journal of Psychiatry, 145,* 584–589.

Lichtenstein, P., Halldner, L., Zettergvist, J., Sjölander A., Serlachius, E., Fazel, S., . . . Larsson, H. (2012). Medication for attention deficit-hyperactivity disorder and criminality. *The New England Journal of Medicine, 367,* 2006–2014. doi:10.1056/NEJMoa1203241

Low, C. (2015). The importance of integrated care and collaborative consultation for advancing early childhood mental health: Lessons learned from professional colleagues. *The Brown University Child and Adolescent Behavior Letter, 31*(2), 1, 6–7. doi:10.1002/cbl.20227

Low, C., & Shepard, S. (2010). Early childhood mental health consultation in early care environments: An introduction. *The Brown University Child and Adolescent Behavior Letter, 26*(3), 1–8. doi:10.1002/cbl.20111

Luby, J., Belden, A., Botteron, K., Marrus, N., Harms, M. P., Babb, C., . . . Barch, D. (2013). The effects of poverty on childhood brain development: The mediating effect of caregiving and stressful life events. *Journal of the American Medical Association, 167*(12), 1135–1142. doi:10.1001/jamapediatrics.2013.3139

Mannuzza, S., Klein, R. G., & Moulton, J. L. (2008). Lifetime criminality among boys with ADHD: A prospective follow up study into adulthood using official arrest records. *Psychiatry Research, 160*(3), 237–246. doi:10.1016/j.psychres.2007.11.003

Maoz, H., Goldstein, T., Goldstein, B. I., Axelson, D. A., Fan, J., Hickey, M. B., . . . Birmaher, B. (2014). The effects of parental mood on reports of their children's psychopathy. *Journal of the American Academy of Child & Adolescent Psychiatry, 53*(10), 1111–1122. doi:http://dx.doi .org/10.1016/j.jaac.2014.07.005

Martell, A. (2013). *Getting Adam back—A mother's triumph over epilepsy & autism.* Amazon Digital Services, Inc.

McLaughlin, K. A., Koenen, K. C., Hill, E. D., Petukhova, M., Sampson, N. A., . . . & Kessler, R. C. (2013). Trauma exposure and post-traumatic stress disorder in a national sample of adolescents. *Journal of the American Academy of Child & Adolescent Psychiatry, 52*(8), 815–830. doi:10.1016/j.jaac.2013.05.011

Meier, M. H., Caspi, A., Ambler, A., Harrington, H., Houts, R., Keefe, R. S., . . . Moffitt, T. E. (2012). Persistent cannabis users show neuropsychological decline from childhood to midlife. *Proceedings of the National Academy of Sciences of the United States of America, 109*(4), 2657–2664. doi:10.1073/pnas.1206820109

Monastra, V. J., Monastra, D. M., & George, S. (2002). The effects of stimulant therapy, EEG biofeedback, and parenting style on the primary symptoms of attention-deficit/hyperactivity disorder. *Journal of Applied Psychophysiology and Biofeedback, 27*(4). Retrieved from http://ashevillebrainbalance.com/wp-content/uploads/2012/02/NEURO FEEDBACK-MED-COMP-MONASTRA1.pdf

Morrow, R. L., Garland, J., Wright, J. M., Maclure, M., Taylor, S., & Dormuth, C. R. (2012, March). Influence of relative age on diagnosis and treatment of attention-deficit/hyperactivity disorder in children. *Canadian Medical Association Journal.* doi:10.1503/cmaj.111619

Olding, S. (2008). *Pathologies: A life in essay.* Calgary, AB: Freehand Books.

Paavonen, J. (2004). *Sleep disturbances and psychiatric symptoms in school-aged children.* Retrieved from http://ethesis.helsinki.fi/julkaisut /laa/kliin/vk/paavonen/. ISBN:952-10-1733-3

Pastor, P. N., Reuben, C. A., & Duran, C. R. (2012). Identifying emotional and behavioral problems in children aged 4-17 years: United States 2001–2007. *Center for Disease Control and Prevention: National Centre for Health Statistics Report, 48.* Retrieved from http://www .cdc.gov/nchs/data/nhsr/nhsr048.pdf

Pathak, P., West, D., Martin, B. C., Helm, M. E., & Henderson, C. (2010). Evidence-based use of second-generation antipsychotics in a state medicaid pediatric population, 2001–2005. *Psychiatric Services, 61*(2), 123–129. Retrieved from http://dx.doi.org/10.1176/ps.2010.61.2.123

Paulson, J., & Bazemore, S. D. (2010). Prenatal postpartum depression in fathers and its association with maternal depression: A meta-analysis. *Journal of the American Medical Association, 303*(19), 1961–1969. doi:10.1001/jama.2010.605

Pelsser, L. M., Frankena, K., Toorman, J., Savelkoul, H. F., Dubois, A. E., Pereira, R. R., . . . Buitelaar, J. K. (2011). Effects of a restricted elimination diet on the behaviour of children with attention-deficit hyperactivity disorder (INCA study): A randomised controlled trial. *The Lancet, 377*, 494–503. Retrieved from http://www.zoelho.com /ZoelhoNL/Publish/Pelsser-The-Lancet-2011-Publication-INCA -study.pdf

Pinquart, M., & Shen, Y. (2011). Behavior problems in children and adolescents with chronic physical illness: A meta-analysis. *Journal of Pediatric Psychology, 36*(9), 1003–1016. doi:10.1093/jpepsy/jsr042

Provenzale, J. M., Isaacson, J., Chen, S., Stinnett, S., & Liu, C. (2010). Correlation of apparent diffusion coefficient and fractional anisotropy values in developing infant brain. *American Journal of Roentgenology, 195*(6), 456–462. doi:10.2214/AJR.10.4886

Rifkin-Graboi, A., Bai, J., Chen, H., Hameed, W. B., Sim, L. W., Tint, M. T., . . . Qiu, A. (2013). Prenatal maternal depression associates with microstructure of right amygdala in neonates at birth. *Biological Psychiatry, 74*(11), 837–844. Retrieved from http://dx.doi.org/10.1016 /j.biopsych.2013.06.019

Rosema, S., Muscara, F., Anderson, V., Godfrey, C., Eren, S., & Catroppa, C. (2014). Agreement on and predictors of long-term psychosocial development 16 years post-childhood traumatic brain injury. *Journal of Neurotrauma, 31*(10), 899–905. doi:10.1089/neu.2013.3226.

Rosler, M., Retz, W., Retz-Junginger, P., Hengesch, G., Schneider, M., Supprian, T., . . . Thome, P. J. (2004). Prevalence of attention-deficit-/hyperactivity disorder (ADHD) and comorbid disorders in young male prison inmates. *European Archives of Psychiatry and Clinical Neuroscience, 254*(6), 365–371. doi:10.1007/s00406-004-0516-z

Safer, D. J., Rajakannan, T., Burcu, M., & Zito, J. M. (2015). Trends in subthreshold psychiatric diagnosis in youth in community treatment. *Journal of the American Medical Association: Psychiatry, 72*(1), 75–83. doi:10.1001/jamapsychiatry.2014.1746

Schreier, A. (2009). *Archives of General Psychiatry, 66*, 527–536.

Shawa, H. E., Abbott, C. W., & Huffman, K. J. (2013). Prenatal ethanol exposure disrupts intraneocortical circuitry, cortical gene expression, and behaviour in a mouse model of FASD. *Journal of Neuroscience, 33*(48), 18893–18905. doi:10.1523/JNEUROSCI.3721-13.2013

Smith, B. H., Molina, B. S. G., & Pelham, W. E. (2002). *The clinically meaningful link between alcohol use and attention deficit hyperactivity disorder.* National Institute on Alcohol Abuse and Alcoholism. Retrieved from http://pubs.niaaa.nih.gov/publications/arh26-2/122-129.htm

Suglia, S. F., Solnick, S., & Hemenway, D. (2013). Soft drinks consumption is associated with behavior problems in 5-year-olds. *Journal of Pediatrics, 163*(5), 1323–1328. http://dx.doi.org/10.1016/j.jpeds.2013.06.023

Swingle, M. K. (2015). *i-Minds: How cell phones, computers, gaming, and social media are changing our brains, our behaviour, and the evolution of our species,* Portland, OR: Inkwater.

Swingle, P. G. (1996). Subthreshold 10Hz sound suppresses EEG theta: Clinical application for the potentiation of neurotherapeutic treatment of ADD/ADHD. *Journal of Neurotherapy, 2*, 15–22.

Swingle, P. G. (2010). *Biofeedback for the brain.* Piscataway, NY: Rutgers University Press.

Tran, A. R., Zito, J. M., Safer, D. J., & Hundley, S. D. (2012). National trends in pediatric use of anticonvulsants. *Psychiatric Services, 63*(11), 1095–1101. Retrieved from http://dx.doi.org/10.1176/appi.ps.201100547

Visser, S. N., Danielson, M. L., Bitsko, R. H., Holbrook, J. R., Kogan, M. D., Ghandour, R. M., . . . Blumberg, S. J. (2013). Trends in the parent-report of health care provider-diagnosed and medicated attention-deficit/hyperactivity disorder: United States 2003-2011. *Journal of the American Academy of Child & Adolescent Psychiatry, 53*(1), 34–46. Retrieved from http://dx.doi.org/10.1016/j.jaac.2013.09.001

Walker, J. E., Normal, C. A., & Weber, R. K. (2002). Impact of qEEG-guided coherence training for patients with a mild closed head injury. *Journal of Neurotherapy: Investigations in Neuromodulation, Neurofeedback, and Applied Neuroscience, 6*(2), 31–42. doi:10.1300/J184v06n02_05

Weitzman, M., Rosenthan, D. G., & Liu, Y. (2011). Paternal depressive symptoms and child behavioral or emotional problems in the United States. *Pediatrics, 128*(6), 1126–1134. doi:10.1542/peds.2010-3034

Yeates, K. O., Bigler, E. D., Dennis, M., Gerhardt, C. A., Rubin, K. H., Stancin, T., Taylor, G., & Vannatta, K. (2007). Social outcomes in childhood brain disorder: A heuristic integration of social neuroscience and developmental psychology. *Psychological Bulletin, 133*(3), 535–556. doi:10.1037/0033-2909.133.3.535

Zito, J. M., Burcu, M., Ibe, A., Safer, D. J., & Magder, L. S. (2013). Antipsychotic use by Medicaid-insured youths: Impact of eligibility and psychiatric diagnosis across a decade. *Psychiatric Services, 64*(3), 223–229. http://dx.doi.org/10.1176/appi.ps.201200081

Index

About the Author

Paul G. Swingle, PhD, RPsych, was Professor of Psychology at the University of Ottawa prior to moving to Vancouver. A Fellow of the Canadian Psychological Association, Dr. Swingle was Lecturer in Psychiatry at Harvard Medical School and during the same time period was Associate Attending Psychologist at McLean Hospital (Boston) where he also was Coordinator of the Clinical Psychophysiology Service. Dr. Swingle was Chairman of the Faculty of Child Psychology at the University of Ottawa and Clinical Supervisor. He has also taught at McGill University, Dalhousie University, and McMaster University. He is a Registered Psychologist in British Columbia and is certified in Biofeedback and Neurotherapy. Since 1997, he has been in private practice in Vancouver, British Columbia, where he founded the Swingle Clinic. His publications include the book *Biofeedback for the Brain* (2010) and his most recent book for professionals, *Adding Neurotherapy to Your Practice* (2015).

Franklin Pierce University

00209432

DATE DUE

PRINTED IN U.S.A.